T0161105

Philosophy in the Garden

Damon Young is a prize-winning philosopher and writer. He is the author or editor of twelve books, including *The Art of Reading*, *How to Think About Exercise*, *Beating and Nothingness*, and *Distraction*. His works have been translated into eleven languages, and he has also written poetry, short fiction, and children's fiction. Young is an Associate in Philosophy at the University of Melbourne.

Philosophy in the Garden

Damon Young

Text illustrations by
Daniel Keating

SCRIBE
Melbourne • London

Scribe Publications
2 John St, Clerkenwell, London, WC1N 2ES, United Kingdom
18–20 Edward St, Brunswick, Victoria 3056, Australia
3754 Pleasant Ave, Suite 100, Minneapolis, Minnesota 55409, USA

Published in North America by Scribe 2020
Published in the UK by Scribe 2019
Originally published in Australia by Melbourne University Press 2012

Text © Damon Young, 2012, 2019
Illustrations © Daniel Keating 2012

All rights reserved. Without limiting the rights under copyright reserved above,
no part of this publication may be reproduced, stored in or introduced into
a retrieval system, or transmitted, in any form or by any means (electronic,
mechanical, photocopying, recording or otherwise) without the prior written
permission of the publishers of this book.

The moral right of the author has been asserted.

While writing this book, Damon Young was an Honorary Fellow of the University
of Melbourne. Publication of this title was assisted by the University of Melbourne,
through The Writing Centre for Scholars and Researchers, and supported by the
Victorian Government through Arts Victoria.

Every attempt has been made to locate the copyright holders for material quoted
in this book. Any person or organisation that may have been overlooked or
misattributed may contact the publisher.

'If it had no pencil' and 'There is a solitude of space' reprinted by permission
of the publishers and the Trustees of Amherst College from *The Poems of Emily
Dickinson; Variorum Edition*, edited by Ralph W. Franklin, Cambridge, Mass.:
The Belknap Press of Harvard University Press, Copyright © 1998 by the President
and Fellows of Harvard College. Copyright © 1951, 1955, 1979, 1983 by the
President and Fellows of Harvard College.

Text design © Melbourne University Publishing Limited, 2012
Typeset by Sonya Murphy

Printed and bound in the UK by CPI Group (UK) Ltd, Croydon CR0 4YY

Scribe Publications is committed to the sustainable use of natural resources
and the use of paper products made responsibly from those resources.

9781950354078 (US edition)
9781912854332 (UK edition)
9781925693867 (e-book)

A catalogue record for this book is available from the British Library.

scribepublications.com
scribepublications.co.uk

Contents

Philosophy Alfresco

Every realm of nature is marvellous ...
    Aristotle, *On the Parts of Animals*

Aristotle had a reputation as a dandy. According to ancient biographer Diogenes Laërtius, the father of scientific philosophy lisped fashionably, and was known for his schmick wardrobe and bling. The impression, bolstered by his ties to the Macedonian royals, is of a metropolitan bon vivant with a taste for opulence. And this makes historical sense: as Aristotle himself noted, philosophy arose in big, rich cities, which gave literate upper classes the leisure to converse and write. But Aristotle's school was not in the Macedonian court, Athens' prestigious suburbs like Kerameikos, or the *agora*, the busy marketplace. The philosopher preferred to give his famous lectures in a park.

His school, the Lyceum, was named for the shaded groves where the philosopher rented his buildings. Situated east of the city walls, the Lyceum was dedicated to Apollo Lyceus, the son of Zeus in his 'wolf god' guise. It had walks, running tracks, change rooms, wrestling schools, temples and *stoa*—porticoes, shaded from sun and rain. Military parades were held there, along with cult rituals. It was an all-purpose reserve for sports, religion, politics—and philosophy. Aristotle taught his students as they strolled around the *peripatoi*, the colonnades—hence their name, the 'peripatetics'. His Lyceum also housed the first botanical garden (probably stocked by the Macedonian empire), which undoubtedly contributed to his lost book *On Plants*.

In this, Aristotle was following his teacher Plato, whose Academy was also in a sacred grove, and who similarly taught on the hoof ('I've been doubting long, and walking up and down like Plato', gibed playwright

Alexis, 'but only tired my legs'). This devotion to gardens lived on in Classical philosophy. Aristotle's own student and successor, Theophrastus, wrote the first systematic treatise on botany, and bequeathed the Lyceum gardens to his colleagues 'as may wish to study philosophy and literature there … on terms of familiarity and friendship'. The Lyceum and Academy schools remained at the heart of Mediterranean intellectual life for over two centuries. One of the great Hellenistic critics of Plato and Aristotle, Epicurus, withdrew to his property in Athens for a life of austere tranquility (and perhaps sour grapes). His school was called 'The Garden': a symbol of his independence, and a means of realising it. 'He who follows nature', Epicurus was quoted by Porphyry as saying, 'is in all things self-sufficient'. Educated Romans also took to gardens for scholarship and conversation, often in a knowing nod to their Greek forebears. Shoved from public office, Cicero wrote of opening an 'Academy' in his own Tusculum villa. He and his students worked while walking outdoors, and Cicero noted the particular joy of watching plants grow. 'I am principally delighted', said Cicero's Cato in 'On Old Age', 'with observing the power, and tracing the process, of Nature in these her vegetable productions'. At the end of the Classical era, over seven hundred years after Aristotle opened his school, the Platonic theologian Augustine was converted to Christianity in a garden. 'I flung myself under a fig tree', he wrote in his *Confessions*, 'and gave free course to my tears'. Philosophy was often alfresco.

There are many reasons for this. Most obviously, gardens are a bulwark against distraction. Philosophy is a gregarious pursuit, which thrives on social ferment. But too much stimulation leads to madness, not meditation. Even in Classical and Hellenistic Greece, cities were noisy, busy and full of interruptions. Athens' streets were small and winding, with residents walking at all hours (often drunk, stumbling home after symposiums). Wagons rumbled and squeaked all day, and if the comic playwright Aristophanes is to be believed, the roads were often dumping grounds for emptied bladders and chamber pots. But Athenians couldn't flee the streets' chaos by heading home, as they often had donkeys, goats and other livestock as housemates. The Lyceum let Aristotle and his students escape the commotion of urban life, and focus on the finer points of logic and metaphysics.

The ancient Greeks were also a physical people, for whom study did not mean a sedentary life. The first schools were gymnasiums for sports like sprinting and wrestling. A public park was a place to stretch their legs, flex their oiled muscles. And gardening itself was, as Socrates reportedly pointed out, an exercise. 'Quite high and mighty people find it hard to hold aloof from agriculture,' he was reported to have said, in Xenophon's *Economist*, 'combining as it does a certain sense of luxury with the satisfaction of an improved estate, and such a training of physical energies as shall fit a man to play a free man's part'.

Aristotle, like many of his students, was also an empirical philosopher. That is, he was not content to merely theorise—he wanted hard evidence. 'Those whom devotion to abstract discussions has rendered unobservant of the facts', he wrote in *On Generation and Corruption*, 'are too ready to dogmatise on the basis of a few observations'. Hence his cultivation of a botanic garden, and his studies abroad. His work on biological classification was detailed, rigorous and unparalleled for millennia—so much so that Charles Darwin referred to the great taxonomists Linnaeus and Cuvier as 'mere schoolboys to old

Aristotle'. For the philosopher, the Lyceum garden was most likely a regular source of philosophical material, for dissection, analysis, synthesis and lecturing—a field trip and laboratory demonstration in one.

Nature and Second Nature

But there are more intellectual reasons for philosophy's *plein-air* tradition. The garden is not simply a retreat or source of physical exercise. It is intellectually stimulating in its own right, because it is a fusion of two fundamental philosophical principles: humanity and nature. This is suggested by the word itself, and its cognates in German and the Romance languages: *Garten, jardin, giardino*. Like the English 'yard', they refer to enclosure, which requires two things: *something* cordoned off (nature), and *someone* to do the cordoning (humanity). Beginning with sacred groves like the Lyceum, every garden is a union of this kind: nature separated, bordered, transformed by humans.

What makes gardens unique is the *explicit* character of this fusion. Nature is regularly and radically transformed by humans. As Aristotle pointed out, this is the very definition of craft: realising natural possibilities that cannot realise themselves. But in art and manufacturing alike, the contributions and combinations of nature and humanity are often hidden. For example, trees become timber; ore becomes metal, zooplankton and algae become oil then plastic—they are natural in origin, but no longer 'nature'. Nature is understood as wilderness, disease, esoteric symbols—as distant 'other'. Meanwhile, human labour is also invisible: we see products and services, but not necessarily the people who produced them. The garden overcomes this double alienation, by displaying human and natural processes together. Plants and stones remain recognisably plants and stones, but they are arranged, cultivated and maintained artfully. In this, they demonstrate our specific relationship with nature—what we *make* of it, physically and intellectually. In the garden, this reality, normally hidden or forgotten, becomes a striking spectacle: a show, a display, a presentation. To use Aristotle's terminology, this primordial relationship is the very possibility that is realised in the garden: it is the demonstration of our physical and intellectual interdependence with nature. The garden makes the humanised cosmos visible and intelligible—a fusion that is seen, felt and thought.

And these two basic principles, humanity and nature, are philosophically provocative. They invite ongoing contemplation, because no final, fixed definition can be given for either.

For example, 'nature' is a deceptively common word—its familiarity masks its plurality and ambiguity. It refers to the whole of reality; to physical things and principles; to life; and to what is easy or customary in humans. Yet even at its broadest, nature is elusive and fundamentally mercurial. As the philosopher Heraclitus put it, a century before Aristotle's birth, '*physis* loves to hide itself'. *Physis* was the Greek word for nature as becoming, which is retained in our 'physics', 'physical' and 'physician'. Nature 'hides itself', in that we are creatures of meaning, but the cosmos is literally meaningless. Talk of 'laws' is misleading, as it implies some cosmic legislator to interpret and re-interpret how things work. Nature has patterns, rhythms and regularities—what philosopher Alfred North Whitehead called its 'temporary habits'. But it has no laws, and no lawmaker; it just is. By contrast, humanity always takes a stance on what 'is' is, consciously or unconsciously. For example, Aristotle saw nature as something of an organism, full of growth and movement. Plato's nature was a divine blueprint, Epicurus' a random strife of atoms. In this way, nature is a philosophical sponge, which absorbs interpretations. But it never does so perfectly, because each interpretation is partial and derivative—and there is always something *more*, beyond our conceptualisations. Partly inspired by Heraclitus' talk of *physis*, the German philosopher Martin Heidegger wrote of human reality as a *Lichtung*, or 'clearing'. It was typical of Heidegger to choose a rustic metaphor, informed by his curmudgeonly anti-modernity. But the metaphor is apt. As *physis*, nature emerges for us, like an illuminated clearing in a dark forest. But the darkness always remains: much of nature withdraws from perception and definition. Reality is less a set of precise axioms or calculations, and more a primordial to-and-fro: nature revealed and concealed, encountered and forgotten, created and annihilated. There is no final word on what nature is—what 'is' is.

Precisely because of this, mankind is also a puzzle. Our existence is enigmatic, because human nature is not universal or eternal, and we are opaque to ourselves. There is not only nature, but also second nature—the first given, the second made. Yet what humanity makes of itself is often unclear and unpredictable. These were the unspoken points of the riddle of the Sphinx, the premise of one of Athens' premier tragedies, Sophocles' *Oedipus Rex*. 'Man' is the answer to the Sphinx's question—'What walks on four legs in the morning, two in the afternoon, and three in the evening, yet keeps its voice?'—but this is a deceptively simple reply. The species continues, but we keep transforming. As individuals and societies, we are works in progress, with novel perspectives and trajectories. And these are rarely completely clear. Poor Oedipus, for all his wisdom, was tragically blind to himself. As Roberto Calasso puts it in *The Marriage of Cadmus and Harmony*, 'the Sphinx hints at the indecipherable nature of man, this elusive, multiformed being, whose definition cannot be otherwise than elusive and multiformed. Oedipus was drawn to the Sphinx, and he resolved the Sphinx's enigma, but only to become an enigma himself'. This is a very modern conclusion, echoing Nietzsche, Heidegger and Sartre. But the suspicion predated Aristotle, and was more forcefully expressed in Greek drama than philosophy: humanity is an ongoing question, not an answer.

These riddles, nature and humanity, combine in the garden. Because of this, it has particular philosophical currency. It can bankroll cosmological and existential ideas, can become invested with historical values, political ideas, domestic rhythms. It is nature humanised. But we also see something beyond ourselves: a hint of an inhuman, unthinking cosmos, which escapes consciousness. This is outside us, in plants' 'hidden life', as Aristotle put it with no small bafflement. But it is also inside us: the dim, blind forces of instinct and habit, which introduce natural necessity into the human psyche. Just as importantly, gardens reveal this intimately and immersively. For all Aristotle's speculative flights, he recognised that humans are embodied creatures: ideas are often inspired and expressed physically. This is doubly so when they are given some organic or primal form, like plants or rocks. The garden gives basic concepts a vital dynamism or dense gravitas.

This intellectual and sensory richness is why gardens still have an air of sanctity to them. Many religious buildings—from the Lyceum's 'wolf god' temples, to

Buddhist monasteries, to medieval cathedrals—have gardens attached or nearby. But these are simply the more notable examples. The garden is not strictly a theistic or spiritual phenomenon. It has its roots in more basic impulses: to carve off a portion of the landscape, and distinguish it from ordinary places. This is suggested by the origins of the word 'sacred': from the Indo-European *sak*, meaning to separate, demarcate, divide. The opposite of the sacred is not the secular but the ordinary, from which it is set apart. In this light, the garden is one of the original sacred sites, preceded by groves like the Lyceum: an area cordoned off from purely natural or human activity, but which explicitly unites both. While perfectly secular, its walls, fences, ditches or hedges symbolise a break from 'common sense'. The garden is, in other words, an invitation to philosophy.

Piety and Strife

This invitation is not only for professional philosophers—as if reflection were a private club for tenured academics. Starting with the Greeks, philosophy has a long amateur tradition, which flourishes as much in literature, poetry and fine art as it does in philosophy seminars. It does not require a university, but rather the balance of society and solitude that universities, at their best, provide. Like Aristotle's Lyceum, the garden is a companion to the life of the mind. Aesthetically, it caters to varied tastes: colourful or muted, geometric or serpentine, busy or austere. But more importantly, in an era of acceleration, overstimulation and interruption, the garden is a chance to slow down, look carefully and think boldly—it is an antidote to distraction. 'The human race lives', wrote Aristotle in

Metaphysics, 'by art and reasonings'. Over two millennia on, the garden remains a rare refuge for both.

Gardens can be beautiful—sometimes overwhelmingly so. They can console, calm and uplift. But they can also discomfit and provoke, and this is often their philosophical value. For all their common themes—order and disorder, growth and decay, consciousness and unconsciousness, stasis and animation—gardens reveal conflict: the conceptual strife in every civilisation, and every civilised mind. For this reason, the story of the garden involves varied characters, with jarring sensibilities. Jane Austen looked to her cottage garden for the comforts of perfection. Leonard Woolf's frozen apple trees suggested exactly the opposite: a taste of the world's precarious brutality. For Marcel Proust, stuck in his musty, latrine-smelling bedroom, three bonsai symbolised a search for lost time. Friedrich Nietzsche's Italian thought-tree gave the sickly philosopher a surge of strength and bravery: forget the past; keep creating and destroying. The scandalous French author Colette discovered contemplative peace in roses. A generation later, her cafe-haunting countryman Jean-Paul Sartre described the nausea provoked by a chestnut tree—an existentialist cry that rallied a generation. In this way, gardens make the truth of philosophical discord easier to identify, and harder to ignore. 'Piety requires us to honour truth', wrote Aristotle in *Nicomachean Ethics*, 'above our friends'. In this spirit, this book is not a tour of 'great estates', but of great minds, and the gardens they loved (and sometimes loathed). It is not a work of philosophy, but a portrait of philosophical lives. The prize they offer is an increased intimacy with nature, human nature, and their mysterious fusion: the garden.

Jane Austen: The Consolations of Chawton Cottage

I am pretty well in health and work a good deal in the Garden.
> Jane Austen, letter to Anna Austen, July 1814

Let us have the luxury of silence.
> Edmund Bertram, in Jane Austen's *Mansfield Park*

It is a May morning in East Hampshire, 1811. Jane Austen's Orleans plums are budding. From her letters and relatives' recollections, I have an imagined portrait of the author, sitting in her favourite spot: near the front door of the cottage, at a small, twelve-sided walnut table, writing on tiny sheets of paper. At the creak of the front door, the pages are tucked away. On this day, her family gives her seclusion, if not quiet. Page after page is filled with her tiny writing: dip, hover, scribble, cross out, scratch and dip. She works quickly, because she has little free time, and concentrates intensely because she has no quiet study of her own. Every so often, she puts down her quill, and conjures up a vision: Fanny Price trembling for the rake Henry Crawford, or stewing over the wickedness of theatre. Then she picks up the pen, and starts again. Eventually the sounds of cooking, cleaning and talk are too much. The plots and subplots of her novel chafe. The clanking pots and servants' chatter are jarring, and her eyes hurt. Enough. Austen puts her pen in the inkwell, and walks out into Chawton Cottage garden.

It is an instant break from the cramped dining parlour. The air is fresher, the light brighter. There is room to move. As her letters record, Austen notices the mock orange's bold white petals and thick, sweet scent. The peony, a recent migrant from Asia, has blossomed again. And what Austen does not see, she anticipates: pinks, sweet Williams, columbines and fat plums. She walks slowly, looks carefully, breathes deeply. But not for too long—Austen has the usual chores and errands for the afternoon, and her unfinished manuscript goads her from

the parlour. But by the time she returns indoors, with her characteristic businesslike step, the garden has already done her good. Jane Austen returns to her tiny work-bench refreshed—not by books or gossip (both in good supply), but by a short holiday amidst Chawton's fruit trees, clipped turf and exotic imports.

With these working habits, Jane Austen wrote her last three novels in about four years—three of the most beloved books in English literature: *Mansfield Park*, *Emma* and *Persuasion*. Despite sickness, domestic duties and the bittersweet ties of family, Austen kept scratching away on her tiny table, creating her incomparable characters.

White Glare

Jane Austen was not always so prolific. Without a garden, her writing suffered. In December 1800, the very month of her twenty-fifth birthday, Austen basically stopped writing for a decade. She penned letters, of course— perhaps thousands, even if we only have a handful now. Nevertheless, her novels were left mostly untouched. She sold *Susan* to a short-sighted publisher, who shelved it (holding it for a £10 ransom). She tried writing a new novel, *The Watsons*, but its gloomy, embittered story went nowhere. From 1800 to 1809, Austen's books disappear from the public and private record. The woman whom literary critic FR Leavis called 'the first modern novelist' was barely writing at all.

Behind Jane's silence was a four-letter word: Bath. In December 1800, her ageing parents announced their retirement: Mr and Mrs Reverend George Austen, and their unmarried daughters Cassandra and Jane, were moving to Bath, on the west coast. Once a Roman resort, and then an English one, Georgian Bath was a brand-new, fashionable holiday destination and health spa. Aristocrats and the rich took vacations there, immersing themselves in the sea, the hot springs and the Pump Room gossip. Architecturally and archaeologically, the city was exciting. Roman ruins and artefacts stood alongside grand new hotels and shops, chiselled from Bath stone. And Bath's urban amenities were balanced by the charm of the local countryside, where a pleasant stroll was never far away—including Prior Park, with its grotto, Palladian bridge and wilderness. 'Bath is the finest place on earth,' wrote Dr Johnson's biographer, the often-pickled whore-hound James Boswell, 'for you may enjoy its society and its walks without effort or fatigue'. For many, Bath was a vibrant, beautiful city, which offered all the modern comforts and amusements, without London's grime and sprawl.

Jane Austen may have enjoyed Bath as a visitor. But as a resident, she hated it. Even in sunshine she thought it ugly. 'The first view of Bath in fine weather does not answer my expectations', she wrote to her sister in her first year in the new town. 'I think I see more distinctly through rain.' She didn't like its ceaseless balls and parties, its flirtatious mood or its stone ('white glare', she dubbed it in *Persuasion*).

Even if Bath had been virtuous and quiet, it was sorely missing one thing: it wasn't *her* town in rural Hampshire, with *her* private garden. It wasn't Steventon, where she was born and raised, and where she wrote her first three novels. Apart from two brief, painful exiles for schooling, Austen had lived for a quarter of a century—her whole life, in other words—in Steventon. A small village surrounded by agricultural land, Steventon was home to perhaps thirty families, alongside the requisite corps of chickens, cows, horses, sheep and pigs. Jane's father, George, was the parson, and schoolteacher to many of the local boys (including five of Jane's brothers). If she was excited by the 'bustle' of a journey west, and the promise of seaside living, Austen still felt a loss.

Country Hampshire wasn't Arcadia: it could be freezing, lonely and dull. No doubt the village's size and isolation occasionally stifled Austen's expansive imagination. Before she left, she wrote to Cassandra, suggesting that her village had grown tiresome to her. But this reads like irony or bravado, not genuine complaint. Steventon was her home, and her archetype of civilised, genteel life. Its intimacy, airiness and domestic rhythms were crucial to her wellbeing. 'The same household routines and daily walks in the garden ... the same sounds and silences', writes her biographer Claire Tomalin, 'all these samenesses made a secure environment in which her imagination could work'.

So part of Jane Austen's silence was undoubtedly shock: the sudden, unavoidable removal of her security. She was accustomed to change: travelling, life's unexpected grief and her parents' economic uncertainty, which she handled with her trademark stoicism. But Steventon was one tangible, familiar constant—the promise of home, after so many trips away. The landscape, neighbours, weather; the familiar walks, visits and conversations; the intricate knot of identity that entangles a place—nothing in polite, modern Bath could measure up to this. The Austens' new terrace house was large, comfortable and located away from the city's thumping heart. But it wasn't Hampshire's agrarian parsonage, and there was no familiar garden to escape to.

While she kept busy with travelling, socialising, bathing or the duties of 'Aunt Jane', Austen lost her voice in Bath—she left it in Steventon, soon occupied by her eldest brother, James, and his second wife, Mary (whom Jane disliked). Her letters, once lively, portray Austen as deflated, if not depressed.

Syringas in Southampton

With the return of a private garden came Austen's familiar energy and productivity. In 1806, she moved with her widowed mother and sister to a new home, Castle Square, in Southampton on the Hampshire coast. Alongside snark and trivia, some of Jane's later letters gleam with enthusiasm for the landscape. She was back on home turf—still maudlin and grumpy, but closer to familiar ground.

In February of the next year, she wrote Cassandra a long epistle, which she hoped was interesting. 'I flatter myself I have constructed you a smartish letter', wrote Austen in her closing lines, 'considering my want of materials, but, like my dear Dr. Johnson, I believe I have dealt more in notions than facts'. For most of the letter, of course, she grumbled. She complained that Cassandra was so long returning to Southampton. She noted that *other* folk were having babies and taking lovers—not her. She carped about sole (or its absence at the markets). And she lamented the loss of shyness in England, replaced by confidence. There's a Pythonesque tone to Austen's letters—as if she were about to burst out with: 'You had fish? Luxury. We had to salt some coal and call it cod'.

But amidst the groaning and bitching is a lovely passage. There is a quiet exuberance, missing in so many of her Bath letters; a playfulness, untinged with cynicism or coolness, suggesting a genuine change of mood. It describes the garden at Castle Square, and it's an arresting glimpse into Jane Austen's inner life. It's worth quoting the 'authoress' (as she called herself) at length:

> Our garden is putting in order by a man who bears a remarkably good character, has a very fine complexion, and asks something less than the first. The shrubs which border the gravel walk, he says, are only sweetbriar and roses, and the latter of an indifferent sort; we mean to get a few of a better kind, therefore, and at my own particular desire he procures us some syringas. I could not do without a syringa, for the sake of Cowper's line. We talk also of a laburnum. The border under the terrace wall is clearing away to receive currants and gooseberry bushes, and a spot is found very proper for raspberries.

Here, Jane's simple, sincere enthusiasm for the garden is endearing: it lacks her characteristic irony, or sharp judgement. With her talk of the syringa, or mock orange, she effortlessly weds William Cowper's poetry ('Laburnum, rich/ In streaming gold; syringa, ivory pure') to the joys of her own backyard. It's joyful and uncomplicated. When she writes of Castle Square's reputation for 'the best Garden in town', her pride is palpable.

This tone of easy delight returned in later letters, once Jane was living in her final home, Chawton Cottage, and working on her last novels. Before settling in the house (which Jane hadn't yet seen), she wrote to her brother about the grounds. 'What sort of kitchen garden is there?' she asked, combining domestic economy with private interest. There was also talk of having the turf 'cropped' before they moved in. In late spring 1811, once settled,

Austen wrote to Cassandra in Kent, giving her a portrait of Hampshire life. Alongside newborns, illnesses, controversial marriages and the weather, she sketched the changes she saw in the garden. The flowers were blooming nicely, but Cassandra's mignonette from Kent had 'a wretched appearance' (Jane frequently made comparisons with her sister—partly because she missed her and perhaps partly out of pride in her own green thumb). The plums were on their way, and Cowper's syringas—obviously planted in Chawton as well as Southampton—were ready to blossom. Austen offers an attractive picture of an English cottage garden in spring. 'Our young Piony at the foot of the Fir-tree has just blown and looks very handsome', she wrote, '& the whole of the Shrubbery Border will soon be very gay with Pinks and Sweet-williams, in addition to the Columbines already in bloom'. Then Austen returns to family journeys, health, the spring storms.

Three years later, staying in her brother Henry's London home, Austen was again struck by the gardens. In 1813, Hans Place was in a rural suburb of London, though hardly provincial—large houses, a good school, and fashionable gardens, all within walking distance of London city (Jane strolled there to do her shopping). Henry Austen's abode wasn't a palace with a large estate, but it was generous (at the time he was a well-to-do banker). His sister commended the house's span and coziness, and then said simply: 'the Garden is quite a Love'.

As with most of Austen's private life, this is little more than a hint: of some more profound human partiality and pleasure. It's difficult to gauge how much of her glee was caused by her removal from Bath—not so much where she was, as where she *wasn't*. Nonetheless, as a reader it's a relief to see Jane Austen so straightforwardly happy.

Despite its vicissitudes, life has mood: themes and tones that colour the years. And the mood of Jane Austen's Bath stay, like her time at boarding school as a child, was one of resigned dissatisfaction. But with the gardens of Castle Square, Hans Place and Chawton Cottage came simple enthusiasm—as if Austen were no longer obliged to suppress her sensual and imaginative delight.

This is why her Chawton talk of mock orange and *Laburnum* stands out. Amidst her usual frustrations and domestic record keeping, it's a sanguine note. When we read of Jane moving her sister's chilled pot plants into the cosy dining room, we can see quiet, domestic enjoyment; the rhythms and gestures that shape everyday life. And we know she was combining these homely, horticultural pursuits with her first love: writing. This is an important clue to Austen's priorities in life. She adored the discipline of writing, but she also saw the garden as vital to her wellbeing. It lifted her spirits, and helped her to write so prolifically. But how?

In High Flutter

A good place to start is with her novels. A caveat, though: Austen was *not* her heroines; not the 'young lady' Sir Walter Scott saw in them. It's convenient to conflate writer and character—particularly intelligent, unmarried gentlewomen of modest means from the provinces. But Austen published six novels in her lifetime, and not one of her heroines can be easily identified with their author. She had Elizabeth's sharp tongue, but not her boldness in company; Elinor's sense, but not her paralysing caution; Catherine's love of literature, but not her Gothicism; Fanny's piety, but not her priggishness; Emma's curiosity for matchmaking, but not her conceited privilege; Anne's loneliness, but not her late romance. In short, Jane Austen did not put herself into *Pride and Prejudice* or *Persuasion*, as if this self were a simple, off-the-shelf phrase or paragraph.

Yet these characters came from *somewhere*: not life, raw and ready-made, but life as ore to be mined, refined, polished. She was not Anne Elliot, with her vain baronet father, or vapid older sister—but she knew enough of repression, disappointment, pride and boredom to imagine Anne's life. The same can be said for her other novels: they were Austen's experiences, skilfully transformed. This is helpful, because it reminds us that the reclusive author, with her many burnt letters, can still be glimpsed in her fiction. Her novels hint at the ideas that informed her writing and life—including her love of Chawton garden.

A good example comes from the world's favourite Austen novel, *Pride and Prejudice*. Jane finished her earliest draft of *First Impressions* at twenty-two years of age. What she thought of it at the time is unknown—she was certainly confident, but this tells us little. Over fifteen years later, after it was published in January 1813 by Thomas Egerton, Austen had mixed feelings. Like most Janeites, she liked her heroine, Elizabeth Bennet. '*I* think her as delightful a creature as ever appeared in print,' Austen told her sister Cassandra in the month of its publication, '& how I shall be able to tolerate those who do not like *her* at least, I do not know'. But she was less sanguine about the virtues of the book as a whole. She recognised its vivacity and charm, but saw it as unserious, and lacking in contrasts. 'The work is rather too light & bright & sparkling', she told her sister. Still, she certainly thought it worthy of publication—even if she didn't put her name to it (the author was 'A Lady'), it was *hers*, faults and all.

What Austen didn't know—as a twenty-something neophyte with a freshly inked manuscript, or as a newly published author—was that *Pride and Prejudice* was to become one of the most popular novels in the English language. It was number one in UNESCO's World Book Day 'books you can't live without' survey, and is a reliable earner for many publishers (Austen outsold John Grisham in 2002). What American author William Dean Howells wrote in 1901 is true today. 'The story of "Pride and Prejudice" has of late years become known to a constantly ... increasing cult', he said in *Harper's Bazaar*. 'The readers of Jane Austen', he continued, counting himself amongst them, 'are hardly ever less than her adorers: she is a passion and a creed, if not a religion' (out soon from Richard Dawkins, perhaps: *The Austen Delusion*).

There are many reasons for the enduring appeal of this book: the wit and intelligent charm of the heroine; the comic bite of the caricatures; the elegance of the prose; the conflicted, frustrated passion of Lizzy Bennet and Fitzwilliam Darcy—coupled with today's drooling over high hats, bushy sideburns and high-waisted dresses. *Pride and Prejudice* lacks psychological nuance, but as a satire, a love story and a sometimes blistering portrait of manners, it is a corker of a novel.

Part of this brilliance is *Pride and Prejudice*'s wonderful set pieces—carefully orchestrated scenes that provide the story with its dramatic turning points—the ball at Meryton, Mr Darcy's first proposal, and Lizzy's confrontation with Lady Catherine de Bourgh, for example. One of the most striking is Elizabeth Bennet's visit to Pemberley, the family home of Mr Darcy (known across the civilised world as the home of Colin Firth's wet shirt). In particular, the gardens of the mansion—described by

Mrs Gardiner, Lizzy's aunt, as 'delightful'—afford Lizzy an opportunity for contemplation.

The story is familiar to all Austen-lovers, but it's worth following the details. On a fine afternoon in Derbyshire, Elizabeth Bennet was excited but apprehensive. In an open-air carriage with her uncle and aunt, the young provincial lady was on her way to Pemberley, the grand estate of the Darcy family. She feigned indifference to the outing. No-one yet knew of Mr Darcy's clumsy marital overtures, so Mr and Mrs Gardiner weren't aware she was 'in high flutter'. And she was trying to be aloof. Darcy was rich, intelligent, handsome and noble—but his pride, and his contempt for her family, rightly incensed her. He had slighted her looks and insulted her with his conceited marriage proposal. 'Could you expect me to rejoice', he fumed, 'in the inferiority of your connections?' Worse still, he had threatened her sister's happiness with his intrusions. To Lizzy and her family, the great Mr Darcy was a stuck-up stick-in-the-mud.

But bit by bit, Elizabeth's resolve was changing. Even as she cursed his 'pride and insolence', she was slowly taking to Darcy. He was honest, forthright and—as she soon discovered—genuinely kind. They shared a keen wit, eloquence and disdain for vulgarity. Despite her misgivings, she was intrigued. Of course she didn't want to meet him, wandering like a tourist on his estate ('She blushed at the very idea'). But he was away for business, and she was free to roam at peace, without fear of embarrassing discovery—or so she thought. As they neared Pemberley, Miss Bennet held her breath, and their carriage slowly drove into the woods.

They drove uphill for a while, the oaks and elms arcing over the carriage. I imagine the trees were hundreds of years old; high, thick branches with generous foliage.

('A beautiful wood, stretching over a wide extent.') While it was cool in the woods, perhaps sunlight sparkled through the leaves. Every now and then, the trees would give way to a set scene: a crisp, clean marriage of grass and water, or a neoclassical temple. After a long drive, they reached the top of the wooded rise, and stopped at a clearing. It was breathtaking, and Elizabeth (like her aunt) was 'delighted'. Pemberley House stood on high ground across from a large stream, in front of forested hills. The pond was teeming with fish, and swans decorated the water. The undulating ground gave the impression of natural landscape, yet it was finer: artful, noble, serene. 'She had never seen', wrote Austen, 'a place for which nature had done more, or where natural beauty had been so little counteracted by awkward taste'. This is partly what changes her mind about Darcy. She sees in the gardens Darcy's soul: expansive, multifarious, but of a piece. And while aroused by its beauty, and a sudden rush of feeling, the heroine's mind is calm, clear. The scales have fallen away. 'At that moment, she felt', wrote Austen, 'that to be mistress of Pemberley might be something!'

It's a well-told story, and Austen handles the dramatic tension brilliantly. But more important is what the author does *not* do in this scene. Given Lizzy's forthright, articulate manner, we might expect a monologue from the heroine: praise, in elaborate Georgian detail, of Pemberley's charms. Of course Elizabeth, like Austen, was no Romantic. But this was Eliza Bennet's great Pemberley epiphany—surely a little gushing was in order?

Not a peep. Despite her 'high flutter', as Austen put it, Lizzy held her tongue. This silence wasn't arbitrary for the author; not a random novelistic detail. And nothing reveals this more keenly than her characterisation of *Pride and Prejudice*'s prize fool, Mr Collins. Elizabeth's unctuous cousin was also a garden-lover. The newly married minister was very proud of his parsonage—its neatness, its nearness to his patroness's estate, and its well-kept grounds. But instead of enjoying it in silence, he was loud, long-winded and pedantic. He would not shut up. He counted the trees, measured the walks and elaborated on every horticultural nicety. 'Every view', wrote Austen, 'was pointed out with minuteness which left beauty entirely behind'. He desperately wanted his companions to praise his garden, in which he'd spent so many days ('one of his most respectable pleasures'). In this, the garden was a stand-in for Collins himself; for his ambitions and expectations. And it was pretty—'large and well laid-out', as the author put it. But Collins' blather obscured this very beauty, just as his vanity and obsequiousness hid the clergyman's better qualities. Despite his Oxbridge education and standing in the community, Collins' verbiage undercut his botanical success and made him look like a idiot.

In this fictional contrast, between her heroine's silence and the parson's talk, Austen offered a fascinating hint of her philosophical interests in the garden. This is the silent, meditative Jane who bent to tend flowers at Castle Square and Chawton; who dutifully rearranged pot plants, ordered Cowper's *Laburnums*, and picked currants and gooseberries. It is an approach characterised by quiet labour and reverie, rather than gossip or chores. And Austen clearly perceived this silence as valuable.

The One Infallible Pope

To understand the silence of Pemberley, it helps to know a little more about Austen's philosophical outlook; about the ideas and intellectual movements that inspired her. The novelist was never a scholar or pamphletist, but she was a prodigious reader. While she has been trivialised as a 'woman writer'—by which critics often disdainfully mean romance authors—she was familiar with a range of scholarly works. Simply because she didn't quote from Robert Henry's *The History of England* does not mean Austen was ignorant of its contents (having read it, the 25-year-old author promised her sister 'a stock of intelligence' when they next spoke). She enjoyed Dr Johnson and his biographer James Boswell, as well as a history of England by Oliver Goldsmith, Johnson's brilliant, vain sparring partner. She also read sermons, praising one Thomas Sherlock to her sister. More surprisingly, we find Austen in 1813 remarking on the entertaining, forceful style of 'An Essay on the Military Police and Institutions of the British Empire', by Captain Pasley. 'The first soldier', she writes to Cassandra from Chawton, 'I ever sighed for'. Clearly, Jane Austen had catholic reading tastes, which touched on history, philosophy, theology, social commentary and the military.

The philosopher Gilbert Ryle speculates that Austen was also influenced by the Fourth Earl of Shaftesbury, the patron and student of Enlightenment luminary Thomas Locke. Shaftesbury's work was shaped by many philosophers, but Aristotle was a particularly important influence. And certainly, Austen's characters—intricate, subtle marriages of vice and virtue—are more reminiscent of Aristotle's morals than the black-and-white ethics of her age's Calvinist theologians (Ryle calls their moral psychology 'bi-polar'). Austen's villainous characters, like Willoughby, are certainly flawed, but not devilish— the dashing young libertine of *Sense and Sensibility* is weak, dishonest and inconstant, but not evil. There are no cardboard-cutout villains in her novels. In the same way, her heroines are not perfect creatures, without shortcomings or errors; from Lizzy Bennet's prejudice to Emma's conceit, Austen gave her women the nuance and variety of genuine human beings. In Austen, there are many moral 'types', rather than simply two camps—Saved and Damned, Good and Bad, Holy and Satanic. This, says Ryle, was Aristotle's outlook, and from him to Shaftesbury. 'Shaftesbury had opened a window', Ryle wrote, 'through which relatively few people in the eighteenth century inhaled some air with Aristotelian oxygen in it. Jane Austen had sniffed this oxygen'. In short, Austen's deceptively simple novels were informed by some of the finest minds of her age: philosophers, essayists, biographers and historians.

But just as influential were the poets. Austen's impressions of right and good conduct were shaped as much by poetry as by systematic thinkers. 'The word "moralist"', Ryle notes, 'would cover Goldsmith or Pope as well as Hutcheson or Hume'. This is particularly true of Alexander Pope, arguably the eighteenth century's greatest—and certainly the most quoted—English poet. His work is less read now, but many of his lines are still familiar proverbs: 'a little learning is a dangerous thing', 'to err is human, to forgive divine', and 'fools rush in where angels fear to tread'. While the two men grated on one another, even the brilliant French dramatist and provocateur Voltaire praised Pope's work. 'The best poet in England', he generously told a correspondent, 'and at present in the world'. High praise from a man who had felt belittled and ignored by Pope. If the poet's ideas were sometimes hackneyed, the formulation was fresh, crisp and biting. Indeed, Pope was here upholding his own definition of 'wit': 'Nature to advantage dress'd;/ What oft was thought, but ne'er so well express'd'. The poet's job was to give ordinary insights new and memorable expression.

In this light, it's no exaggeration to say Pope dressed the thought of the Anglophone eighteenth century, including that of Jane Austen. Like Shaftesbury and Austen, Alexander Pope was in the Aristotelian tradition: more interested in human variety than the Calvinist battle for souls. He saw character as subtle, various and fickle. While each man had a 'ruling passion', all was change: 'Manners with fortune, humours turn with climes', he wrote in a letter to Lord Cobham, 'tenets with books, and principles with times'. Accordingly, Austen quoted Pope in two of her novels, *Northanger Abbey* and *Sense and Sensibility*, and in a letter to Cassandra, she joked that he was 'the one infallible Pope in the world' (ironic, given his Catholicism). In the same letter, Austen used the poet to demonstrate her own stoicism. 'Whatever is, is best', she wrote, poignantly paraphrasing a line from Pope's moral poem 'An Essay on Man'.

And it is Pope's 'Essay' that gives an outline of Austen's unarticulated (but by no means inarticulate) philosophical worldview. Like Austen, Pope's starting point was simple: man's ignorance. By this, he didn't mean just misinformation or inaccuracy—the sort of ignorance overcome by fact checking or detective work. Instead, Pope was talking about the basic limitations of human perception and knowledge. Whereas God sees and knows all, he argued, we can only ever know a tiny portion of our tiny world (let alone the cosmos); we are petty, small, vulnerable and easily confused creatures. Pope's God has a magisterial grasp of the whole, while humankind clumsily clings to a part: a little patch of earth, and an even smaller snatch of eternity.

Perhaps more importantly, Pope said there's little point in questioning this cosmos. First, he argued, our ignorance makes any exhaustive answer impossible. We can no more understand the cosmos than an ox can the farmer's agricultural plan—like the ox, we are simply not up to it. Second, even if we *were* to miraculously comprehend the universe in its totality, it would be foolish and futile to expect anything to change. 'Of systems possible it is confess'd', wrote Pope, 'that Wisdom infinite must form the best'. In short, we have the finest cosmos possible. From our bounded horizons, things might *seem* ugly, unjust or unreasonable, but actually it's a balanced, harmonious system; an infinitely precise means, working toward His divine ends. Every species of mite, bird and mammal is an instrument in this symphony, but none, save the maestro, knows the grand dénouement. And to want to alter our part is absurd and dangerous, for the tiniest discordance or missed beat ruins the composition. Imagine the universe as an exquisite, delicate music box, with countless gears, wheels, springs: the slightest damage ends the song. 'From Nature's chain whatever link you strike', he wrote, 'tenth, or the tenth thousandth, breaks the chain alike'. This is a perfect, unified, rational harmony. In Pope's world, all is as it should be, as it *must* be.

For the poet, this had a clear moral lesson: enough of the speculation and lamentation; just get on with life. Of course we might rail against privation, or rage against slights; we might regret lost chances, or be fearful of the future. But all in all, we have precisely the power, authority and capacity we should have—and all of the world's forces are competing and colluding to produce a stable, law-like cosmos. We can't interrogate it, or change a single letter or line of the blueprint; it all stands, universal and eternal. Better to give up on cosmic conceit and get on with the business of human life, with our everyday victories and defeats. This is the source and sense of Jane Austen's misquoted phrase, in her letter to Cassandra. 'Spite of pride, in erring reason's spite', wrote Pope, 'one truth is clear, Whatever is, is right'. Austen's credo, via the poet, was a simple but powerful one: all's well up there, so save your energy for down here.

If the theology is suspect, there are, nonetheless, several bold ideas in this cosmology, which resonate with Jane Austen's moral universe. Most obviously, Pope was suggesting that there's no point taking issue with the facts of physics or biology, or worrying about the grand 'why' of the universe. Better to take care of our families, be loyal to our friends and leave something beautiful or useful behind us when we die. More crucially, Pope was arguing that the scope and scale of this human life is worthwhile; that we have our allotted powers and potential, and they are a valuable part of a beautiful whole.

Common to Pope and Austen was this combination of enthusiastic worldliness and quiet, consoled faith. Like the poet, Austen read broadly, and with a sharp eye for detail and an ear for style. But she was no metaphysician: the sublime intricacies of Leibniz's 'best of all possible worlds' were beyond her interest, if not her comprehension. She believed in a cosmic order—and had no wish to probe or overthrow it. 'Religion is there', writes Claire Tomalin in her sparkling Austen biography, 'an essential part of the fabric of her life. It was never something to be questioned or investigated ... more of a social than a spiritual factor'. Behind Austen's literary marriages, families, and portraits of virtue, and upholding her own perseverance and patience, was faith in the order of things. This is precisely why the author could focus on her domestic squabbles, romantic intrigues and economic struggles: they were her domain of sympathy, aspiration and knowledge. Pope's striking lines capture this entirely:

Know then thy self, presume not God to scan,
The proper study of mankind is Man.
Placed on this isthmus of a worldly state,
A being darkly wise, and rudely great.

In this crisp portrait of humanity's alloy, we have Austen's flawed characters and familiar plots, and her own quiet faith in a world beyond her own rural England. Her novels *were* this 'proper study'.

Tolerable Comfort

This calmative is what Lizzy Bennet quietly savoured at Pemberley. Not its promise of wealth and status, but its quiet representation of harmony and order. It reminded the anxious young woman that her world, with all its grief and worry, was not everything; that there was dignity, restraint and grace in nature—the virtues she also saw in Darcy.

What Austen put into *Pride and Prejudice*, she herself experienced in Chawton, Castle Square and her Steventon acres. She could endure the draining vicissitudes of family and art—from boredom to grief to elation and back—and then withdraw to Southampton's *Laburnum*, or Chawton's beech. Regardless of siblings' squabbles, the threat of war with the French or the stubbornness of a character who will not 'fit', the bulbs still flowered every spring. 'I hear today', wrote Austen to her sister on the last day of May 1811, 'that an Apricot has been detected in one of the Trees'. This is more than another trivial fact; more than gossip or mild amusement. It is a nod to the eternal signs of life. In Chawton's garden, Austen could encounter Pope's perfect cosmos: a reality less ambiguous, flawed and transient than that of human affairs. It reaffirmed her quiet faith—that permanent backdrop behind the foreground action.

If Austen could be unsentimental in her letters, she was certainly willing to be comforted. 'Let other pens dwell on guilt and misery', she wrote famously in *Mansfield Park*. 'I quit such odious subjects as soon as I can, impatient to restore everybody … to tolerable comfort.' Even allowing for the usual pinch of Austen irony, she was serious: her published novels always pursued happy endings, in which even Marianne Dashwood gets her colonel. Despite her recognition of psychological, social and economic reality, the novelist was happy to seek and offer consolation: 'tolerable comfort' in Pope's metaphysical guise. Austen was rediscovering what the theologian Augustine described as 'occasions when human reason is nearer to some sort of converse with the nature of things': sowing seeds, planting cuttings, grafting slips. Chawton Cottage garden was a lesson in what's now called 'the big picture'—but Jane Austen savoured it on a smaller scale.

Marcel Proust:
Bonsai in the Bedroom

*Those Japanese dwarf trees ... if I arranged a few of
them beside a little trickle of water in my room I should
have a vast forest, stretching down to a river, in which
children could lose their way.*

    Albertine, in Marcel Proust's *In Search of Lost Time*

*I still have three miserable hideous little Japanese
trees to give you. Having seen them announced at a
sale, I sent my pseudo-secretary to buy them. What a
disappointment when I saw them! However, they will
get to be nice, and they are so old and little.*

  Marcel Proust, letter to Madame Straus, 21 June, 1907

Save for a long-stemmed bedside lamp, the bedroom on
the first-floor apartment was dark: shutters closed, blue
satin curtains drawn. A small brass bed was blanketed
with pages, each covered with wayward, seismogram
handwriting. In a thick, black beard, and wrapped in

woollen underwear, white pyjama top and coarse socks, was Marcel Proust—not quite famous, but well on his way. The young author, not yet thirty-six, was breathing scratchily, his chronic asthma worsened by the room's dust and the filth of his sheets ('far from clean', as biographer Richard Barker diplomatically wrote). Perhaps the room stank of old food and urine—'jam pots and chamber pots', as his friend Robert de Montesquiou put it, with characteristic bitchiness. Perhaps the bedroom was still dirty from the collapse of his chimney, days earlier. Unharassed by the violating light of the sun, that 'very beautiful and very strange object', as he called it, Proust was ready for work.

On this cold March night in Paris, 1907, Proust was not yet writing his magnum opus, *A la Recherche du Temps Perdu* (usually translated as *In Search of Lost Time*, or *Remembrance of Things Past*). Instead, he was writing a review of a friend's book of poetry: *Dazzlings*, by the Comtesse Anna de Noailles. He had only just read his copy, mailed to him a day or so earlier by Noailles.

Marcel had little trouble recognising or describing the poet's achievements, rating her with Olympians like Voltaire, Victor Hugo and Arthur Baudelaire (history did not agree). The first draft of his review was written in three hours—some sixteen thousand words by his reckoning, which he spent the next three months cutting down, hoping to get it published on the front page of *Le Figaro*. To no avail—shorn, the final copy was published in mid-June, tucked away in *Le Figaro*'s literary supplement ('A foretaste of eternal oblivion', Proust said). Nonetheless, Marcel's review was sober and revealing. While he had not yet discovered the memorial magic of *In Search of Lost Time*, his analysis of Noailles' poems

shows a great mind humming the first bars of its legend-
ary *idée fixe*: the rediscovery of the past in small details.
In this review, as in his essays and literary parodies,
Marcel the idling dilettante was becoming that mysterious creature of myth and dissertation: Proust, the great
modern author.

Beside him as he wrote were three 'miserable, hideous' Japanese bonsai, as he described them, which he
had sent his young secretary, Robert Ulrich, out to pur-
chase. Characteristically put out by departures from his
taste, Proust thought them ugly, and later sold them to
his friend Madame Straus. But they were by no means
useless to the author, playing an important role in his
Noailles review. And what they suggested to Proust was
central to his celebrated vision of life and art.

'A Lot of Japs'

Bonsai were quite fashionable at the turn of the century: part of the *japonisme* fad that invaded France and England. After Commodore Perry and his 'black ships' threatened feudal Japan into trade and military relations, the West was slowly introduced to Japanese aesthetics and philosophies. While Japanese youths wore three-piece suits, bowler hats and wristwatches, the painter James McNeill Whistler donned a kimono, slept on a futon and ate with chopsticks. 'We are leading an impossible life,' wrote French painter Henri Fantin-Latour from London in July 1864, 'all three of us, in Whistler's studio. We might be at Nakasaki'. Like Proust, Whistler was friends with Robert de Montesquiou and his aesthete clique ('a lot of Japs', snapped a disapproving aristocrat). Many Art Nouveau artists, for whom Whistler was an important precursor, were also fascinated by Japanese woodblock prints, iconography and colouring techniques. Indeed, the source of Proust's bonsai, Bing's studio and workshop, was also the source of the name of the 'new art' movement—'L'Art Nouveau Bing', 22 Rue de Provence, Paris. And pre-Impressionists like Degas and Manet, and Impressionists like Monet, were also enamoured of Japanese craftsmanship and artistry. Japan and *japonisme* were at the heart of fin-de-siècle artistic innovation and experimentation.

For his part, Proust was intrigued by the Japanese talent for suggestion, simplicity and subtlety; for immensity suggested by a few crisp lines, or richness evoked in miniature workmanship. A close friend, Marie Nordlinger, worked at the Art Nouveau workshop, and was a direct source of Japanese artistry for him. Nordlinger remembered Marcel, in bed, gazing at her Japanese cloisonné earrings, with their intricate painting and glaze. 'May I touch them? Don't take them off!' In April of 1904, Nordlinger gave Proust a more significant Japanese miniature: tiny pellets of dried pith, which, when wet, unfurled into flowers, trees and animals. Proust, whose asthma robbed him of his beloved countryside, was able to imagine his way into a blooming garden. 'Thanks to you', he wrote to Marie, 'my dark electric room has had its Far-Eastern Spring'. This transformation appeared again in the celebrated description of cake dipped in tea, which triggered the memories of his childhood. The passage from *Swann's Way* (the first volume of *In Search of Lost Time*) is a paean to the magic of Nordlinger's Japanese gift:

> Just as the Japanese amuse themselves by filling a porcelain bowl with water and steeping in it little crumbs of paper which ... the moment they become wet, stretch themselves and bend, take on colour and distinctive shape, become flowers or houses or people, permanent and recognisable, so in that moment all the flowers in our garden and in M. Swann's park, and the water-lilies on the Vivonne and the good folk of the village and their little dwellings and the parish church and the whole of Combray and of its surroundings, taking their proper shapes and growing solid, sprang into being, town and gardens alike, from my cup of tea.

The very Proustian point is clear: from tiny things, grand memories and fantasies unfold.

This was a vital theme in Proust's literary work. In his review of *Swann's Way*, writer Jean Cocteau wrote of Proust's painterly gift for artfully compressing characters, social observations, landscapes into delicate details. 'Swann is a gigantic miniature', he wrote, 'full of mirages, superimpositions of gardens, plays as space and time, broad cool touches in the style of Manet'. This talent was also recognised by Proust's biographer George Painter. In a particularly moving passage of his *Marcel Proust*, Painter revealed the author's genius for capturing the vital essence of an age and class; for portraying, in small details, the unique character of the fin-de-siècle aristocracy, annihilated in World War I. Hence Proust's interest in bonsai, alongside Japanese earrings, woodblocks and toys. Like his magnum opus, Proust's bonsai were a salute to the vastness evoked by small things.

Uncoincidentally, this was exactly how Proust characterised Noailles' poems on that March night, writing with the three bonsai at his bedside. In his *Figaro* review, he examined the poet's talent for alluring images and metaphors from her past—what Proust called 'the resurrection of what we have felt'. Fish became swallows, magpies became fruit. Noailles reached beyond the world of bare stuff, toward the poetic repository of the past. 'She knows', wrote Proust, 'that a profound idea which has time and space enclosed within it is no longer subject to their tyranny, and becomes infinite'.

'... In My Room I Should Have a Vast Forest'

In this light, the bonsai were no mere coincidence or fashionable impulse buy—as if Proust had gone shopping for exercise books but had returned with a stunted cherry tree. The bonsai were in keeping with an ongoing preoccupation of the author: they were small inscriptions offering immense visions. This was both a literary hall-mark of Proust, and a fascination in his life.

Proust did not explore precisely *how* the bonsai accomplished their magic. But the important qualities are not difficult to note: they are a combination of immediacy, availability, distillation and beauty or striking form. Bonsai offer the subtle intricacy of an everyday tree, but in a small, intimate size. The bonsai also has a unique relationship to temporality. While the old bonsai, with its often gnarled branches and tortured shapes, evokes age and suffering, it achieves this by defying the signs of time. Its roots, leaves and branches are trimmed and trained into definite shapes and patterns. Perhaps it changes pots, or is moved from its porch stand to a niche indoors; perhaps it flowers in spring, and reddens in autumn. But the nature of the bonsai is stillness and sameness. As Deborah Koreshoff puts it in her classic *Bonsai*, 'what has attracted you is the FORM and STYLE … the "bones of the design"'. It is something of a type, from the Greek *typos*: a stamp. Because of this, the bonsai can be many trees: by epitomising their basic character, it suggests a certain archetypal 'treehood', common to all. The bonsai refines experience as it simplifies it. And it often does so beautifully, with the kind of delicacy and intricacy Proust admired in Japanese woodblock prints and cloisonné earrings. Part garden, part sculpture, the dwarf tree contains grandeur and flux in a single, simple and lasting design.

This is why Proust told Marie Nordlinger that bonsai were 'trees for the imagination'. Just as a seed prompts us to imagine a future flower, argued Proust, so too does the bonsai prompt the dream of some melancholy landscape, with its mournful epochs. These are the 'centuries old dreams, the expanse and the majesty of a great field', and for all their ugliness, they captured his imagination. It is the poetic outlook behind the words he gave to Albertine in *In Search of Lost Time*. 'Those Japanese dwarf trees which one feels are still cedars, oaks, manchineels', she says to the narrator Marcel, 'so much so that if I arranged a few of them beside a little trickle of water in my room I should have a vast forest, stretching down to a river, in which children could lose their way'. In this fantasy, bonsai are not simply small trees, pot plants or symbols of exotic Japan; they are a typically Proustian device: invitations to dream of immensity and age.

Return from Exile

Proust's attraction to suggestive miniatures was both biographical and philosophical. With his interest in tiny things in general, and the bonsai in particular, Proust was not merely after literary technique. He was also seeking recompense for, and recovery of, what he had lost in life: a kind of metaphysical whole denied by age and infirmity. His obsessive pursuit occurred not in grand tours or textbooks, but in the realm of small, unobtrusive things.

One reason for this was illness. Proust was alienated from the natural world, and his bonsai offered him the consolation of an imaginary countryside. While his hermetic later life suggested otherwise, Proust learnt to love the outdoors early. As a child at Auteuil and Illiers, he was besotted with grasses, breezes and the green canopy above. At Illiers, Proust's maternal uncle Jules owned three gardens: a small backyard, a vegetable patch and a pleasure garden, Pré Catalan. Pré Catalan offered the young Proust lawns, palm trees, geraniums and a pond bordered by irises and forget-me-nots, decorated by swans and waterlilies. On the edge of the garden, a hedge of pink and white hawthorns—the first was Marcel's favourite, reminding him of pink iced biscuits, and crushed strawberries with creamed cheese. At Auteuil, with his Great-Uncle Louis' house 'as tasteless as it could possibly be', Marcel sat under tall trees and walked with his family by the Bois de Boulogne. Alongside his more beloved hawthorn, there were chestnut trees, 'a youthful breed of giants which', he wrote in *Jean Santeuil*, 'wear their high blossom like massive, delicate towers'. Proust's childhood had a rustic, dreamlike quality, which fuelled the writer's work.

This idyll didn't last. As a middle-aged man, he still loved flowers, telling his housekeeper Céleste to look more closely at hawthorn—'I don't know of anything prettier', he said. But the charms of Auteuil, Illiers and springtime were lost to the chronic asthmatic. Instead of enjoying spring's wildflowers, Proust had to sit mournfully inhaling Legras powder. Céleste's husband, Odilon, would sometimes drive their employer to the Chevreuse Valley to see hawthorn and apple trees in blossom—but Proust was always locked behind the safe, sealed glass of the car. Before he retreated entirely into sickness and writing, Proust visited his old servants, who were in a home. He stood outside by a bed of pansies, and sniffed *one* happily in his hand. 'The only flower I can smell without getting asthma', he told his friend. Middle-aged Proust loved the countryside, but was almost always parted from his beloved (unreachable love: another Proustian theme).

This distance gave added charm to his bonsai: they were genuine trees, alive in his bedroom. Ugly as they were, he prized them, because they re-introduced the living landscape to his sickroom. Nothing could replace the vistas of Auteuil and Illiers, chestnuts, carp-filled water and hedges. But Proust's bonsai were a prompt to re-invent lost landscapes, after years of exile—a brief reclamation of lost childhood.

In Search of …

But alongside this more immediate biographical motive was a second rationale, bound up with Proust's distinct philosophical outlook. He did not simply seek to regain his own past—his ideas had a more general relevance. He believed that tiny things and subtle details could be pathways to a richer, broader consciousness. This idea was at the heart of Proust's mature philosophy.

It might seem out of place to talk of Proust as having a 'philosophy'. After all, many thought Proust incapable of deep thought. Well into middle age, he was caricatured as a sycophant, dilettante and socialite—a man without talent, discernment or intellectual clarity. The publishing house Nouvelle Revue Française rejected the first volume of his novel, dismissing him as, in Andre Gide's words, 'a snob, a literary amateur'. Gide and his colleagues later recanted with a generous apology and contract. But their original impressions are telling: Proust was seen as a gifted but shallow dandy, all polish and no stone. Perhaps he was amiable and eccentric, but, went the received wisdom, he was too much of a hypochondriac, poseur and idler to write anything truly great. And even if his stories or reviews were charming, they did not have the profundity or clarity expected from genuine philosophy. His mimicry, fashionable parties and aesthetic clique all screamed shallowness and degeneracy. To many peers, Proust was a brightly coloured parrot.

Posterity has treated him with more respect: the 'great philosophical novelist', writes his American biographer Edmund White. While by no means an academic, Proust certainly enjoyed philosophy at the liberal Condorcet school, where he studied from the age of eleven to seventeen. Proust was a capricious student, and his lessons were often interrupted by illness—he did not always excel early on. Nonetheless, Marcel was intelligent, sincere and passionate, virtues at home in philosophy. In his final year at Condorcet, he started *philosophie* with Marie-Alphonse Darlu, labelled 'that Great philosopher' by Proust in his *Pleasures and Days*. Sarcastic but genuinely dedicated to philosophy, and the teaching of it, Darlu honed the young Proust's ideas and cultivated his love for the deeper significance of things.

As the course was chiefly based on the ideas of Immanuel Kant, we might say that Proust was taught not simply of things, but of things in themselves: *the* real world, beyond our immediate, idiosyncratic perceptions. Kant's basic idea was that we can understand the world because, as we perceive it, it is largely the work of our minds. The reason the universe seems rational is not because there is some divine mind pulling strings, but because we impose order upon experience. Kant called this the 'phenomenal' realm: the world of human perception. Opposed to this was the 'noumenal' world: not things as they appear to us, but things in themselves. The noumenal world is real; it is the 'stuff' that the human mind works upon. But we have no direct access to it: by the time we are seeing and thinking, the things in themselves are already humanised. The upshot of Kant's theory is, first, a very rigorous education in intellectual categories, and in their relation to morality and aesthetics, and, second, the impression of a grand netherworld that is tangible but unknowable—a 'true reality', from which we are exiled.

Proust took naturally to this idealistic, almost mystical theory and named Darlu as one of his 'heroes in life'. The bright young Marcel was never to be a professor of philosophy—his talents lay elsewhere. Nonetheless, Proust was always marked by his study with Darlu and later returned to private lessons with the professor. Years later, as he grimly finished his law degree at the Sorbonne, he was still confessing his love for literature and philosophy. Anything else, the 22-year-old told his father, was '*temps perdu*': time lost.

Darlu's lessons provided some form for the later psychological substance of Proust's novels and stories. 'It is the Spirit', wrote the young Proust, 'that structures matter'. The world we know, in other words, is one our minds delineate and organise—'we can reduce', he continued, 'matter to psychological elements'. But however intricately reality is built to the mind's blueprint, there is always *something* beyond—some greater, more ancient and perfect truth. This is Proust's melancholy metaphysics: there is a whole, of which we are one lonely, longing part.

Later, in the prologue to his collection of essays *Contre Sainte-Beuve*, written as he worked toward *In Search of Lost Time*, Proust explored this idea more maturely: that there is some wonderful 'beyond', waiting for us in the ordinary world. To begin, for Proust the most valuable thing was the past. As Painter argued in his biography of the author, the past was more than lost time to Marcel. Instead, it represented a time of innocent, naïve wholeness—a kind of ideal, eternal unity, over and above the grief, conflict and confusions of adulthood.

'In this momentary but endless admission to the world beyond time lies salvation', Painter explained, 'since there alone is the virtue we lose when we are born, and the joy which earthly love can take away'.

But, wrote Proust, this enchanting past is lost to us daily: first, because the mind is too diluted or distracted to notice it at the time and, second, because the intellect cannot do it justice. In other words, the past is forever slipping away, impossible to fix. Time lived is time lost. 'Several summers of my life', Proust wrote crisply in his *Sainte-Beuve* prologue, 'were spent in a home in the country. I thought of those summers from time to time, but they were not themselves. They were dead'. For Proust, there *is* a world of eternal beauty and love, where the perfect and painless 'beyond' endures. But it is unobtainable, leaving most of us chronically dissatisfied. Proust believed this was the quintessential human condition: locked out of the storehouse of memory.

Yet the door is always ajar, says Proust—the past is locked up in everyday things, waiting to be freed. 'In reality, as soon as each hour of one's life has died', he wrote in *Contre Sainte-Beuve*, 'it embodies itself in some material object ... and hides there'. This is Proust recalling a garden in a cup of tea or Venice in a loose stepping stone. But it is not enough to simply access those memories, he argued; we need to recognise and reclaim them. In other words, once memory returns, it requires conscious, creative attention. Proust's dictum: first accident, then art.

The Fugitive Rescued

This is Proust's famous theory of 'involuntary memory'. In the clear, unpretentious prose of his *Sainte-Beuve* prologue, he articulated the vastness of the accumulated past, and the impossibility of faking or falsifying it. The past cannot be grasped in abstract thoughts, or cobbled together from half-forgotten fragments. Like finding old coins in the pocket of an unworn jacket, these treasures can only be happened upon. Then they must be recognised and consciously elaborated on.

In this, Proust was shooting across the bow of over-confident rationalism—the belief that the mind is absolutely transparent to itself; that the most civilised and sophisticated impressions are all amenable to consciousness. Recollection, Proust was arguing, is at the whim of chance and opaque, unconscious impulses. Our minds are precarious, murky and fleeting. And not even the most revered signposts from our past, like a cherished family home or childhood park, can anchor us. 'The memory of a particular image is but regret for a particular moment', wrote Proust in the moving last lines of *Swann's Way*, 'and houses, roads, avenues are as fugitive, alas, as the years'.

Interestingly, this theory is also an attack on snobbery, for which Proust was himself renowned. For if our past is safe-kept in seemingly mundane things, then the commonplace can be more valuable to the artist than lauded museum pieces or collectibles. Of course, Proust was not disavowing the glories of Amiens cathedral, Saint-Saëns' sonatas or Vermeer's *View of Delft* ('the most beautiful painting in the world', which the ailing author braved vertigo and dizziness to see). He had a responsive, fervent and enduring love of art. But alongside this, he recognised the worth of the unrefined and the ordinary. 'A book that means nothing to people of discrimination but is full of names he has heard since he was a child', Proust wrote of the artist in *Contre Sainte-Beuve*, 'can be worth incommensurably more to him than admirable philosophical treatises'.

This was Proust's more ambitious point, which explains the value of the bonsai: in the humble and overlooked, he hoped to encounter the worlds—vast or forgotten—he lost daily. In miniatures or small details, he was illuminating murky parts of the mind, or making fresh connections between seemingly disparate facts, feelings and memories. The bonsai sitting by his bedside, then, were not only a return to lost nature, on a domestic scale. They were also an emblem of a more ambitious project: the recovery of Proust's 'fugitive', his life.

Rediscovery

Reading Proust's life story, the oddness of it all is striking. Perhaps the hat-pinned rats and neurotic mother-love can be dismissed as the fictions of gossip-hounds and biographers (though the psychological shoes do fit). Even without these, it is difficult to relate to Proust. There is a logic to his airless seclusion and nostalgia, but it is absurd. As a middle-class Jew I can see the allure, for Proust, of easy, elegant aristocrats, who simply *belonged*. For all his gifts, he was an outsider. As a writer, I recognise the importance of privacy and silence. As a parent, I sympathise with the theme of childhood lost. But there is a mysterious covetousness to Proust—a grasping, needy, desperate quality to him—which I simply cannot fathom. He is like an obscure foreign language, understood only abstractly in translation. Proust was an uncommon man—a man of rare genius and idiosyncratic psychic architecture. I am not at home in his world, and I suspect I am not alone in this.

Nonetheless, the ideas that Proust saw in his bonsai are distinctive and valuable. His example confirms once again that gardens need not be grandiose and expensive—in fact, they need not be gardens at all. Not everyone has the hours, dollars or knack to cultivate Pré Catalan; not everyone has the lungs or nimble fingers to make their hawthorns thrive. But what Proust achieved in his dark bedroom can be mirrored in poky rented flats or paved backyards. The principle of the bonsai works for olive trees in a courtyard, or potted geraniums on a porch. Austerity of landscape does not mean poverty of mind.

Proust's bonsai philosophy also makes a broader point. It is a simple but direct call to take notice of, and to celebrate, the most ordinary stuff of life. It is, in other words, a warning against the anaesthesia of familiarity. Small details, tiny things, half-seen instances, can offer surprising insights and impressions if we look closely enough. This is, first, in the craftman's sense: decades of clipping, pruning and wiring offer the gardener the pleasures of mastery, preoccupation and beauty (or clumsiness, confusion and dead saplings, in my case). Second, it rewards in the art-lover's sense: intricate, delicate, graspable things can be more enriching than their size suggests. This is the lesson of Proust's 'miserable, hideous little trees', but it is also a habit of curious, unhurried consciousness. The bonsai is a living reminder: to rediscover the miniature universes that hide in plain sight.

Leonard Woolf: The Apples of Monk's House

Pruned trees and my finger. Rain & wind.
> Leonard Woolf, letter to Lytton Strachey,
> 24 January 1920

NOTHING MATTERS.
> Leonard Woolf, letter to Molly MacCarthy,
> 17 June 1921

In a sharp, unforgiving Sussex winter, a wiry man pruned apple trees, and tied plums to the wall. He was wearing two pairs of socks, gloves and two jackets, to no avail—the chill still bit at his bones. As he approached middle age, he increasingly felt the cold. And those January days were, his wife said, 'like frozen water, ruffled by the wind into atoms of ice against your cheeks'.

But Leonard Woolf kept at it. In fact, he had worked like an eager schoolboy since he and Virginia had bought Monk's House at auction, just over six months earlier. The Woolfs were mad about the property. It was not the house that first seduced them, with its scattering of out-houses and harvest sheds. Having bicycled to Rodmell a week before the sale, Virginia was reserved and critical about Monk's House. It had small, cluttered rooms, no hot water, an old oil stove, a damp kitchen and a small larder. And, they later learnt, it flooded. But Virginia's interest was quickly kindled by the 'profound pleasure' of the garden: rows of fruit trees, peas, artichokes, potatoes and raspberries; a soothing roll and rise of lawn, offering shelter from storms; all in all, 'size & shape & fertility & wilderness', and all theirs for the price of a used Volvo today. On the day of the sale, Leonard quietly, nervously gripping £800 in his pocket, tried to be cautious, but the couple were unalterably excited ('I was purple in the cheeks', wrote Virginia, '& L. trembling like a reed').

Seemingly to her own surprise, Virginia Woolf enjoyed gardening. At first she thought her chief amusement would be walking: over the Rodmell countryside when the days were warmer, then in the sheltered grass when the merciless winds set in. She was, she suggested in her diary, more of a wanderer, a gaper than a landscaper. Her walks gave her the 'raw material' of her novels. 'All the time on the downs, across the water-meadows, or along the river bank', wrote Leonard in *Downhill All the Way*, 'in the front or at the back of her mind was the book or article she was writing or the embryo of a book or story to be written'. And conversational, countryside walks were something she and Leonard could enjoy together. Early on at Rodmell, the Woolfs strictly timetabled their strolls, in case they spent more time by the Ouse River than writing.

But by the next year, Virginia Woolf was more taken with the garden itself. The daffodils shone; crocuses rose from their bulbs, and almonds blossomed ('SPRING', she wrote that March, with happy capitals). By May, the seemingly aloof author spent one warm but breezy afternoon on her hands and knees, getting filthy. 'Weeding all day to finish the beds', she wrote in her diary, 'in a queer sort of enthusiasm which made me say that this is happiness'. Her office was a room in the garden—once a tool shed, then a study, with storage for apples.

Over the next fifty years, however, it was Leonard who was wedded to lawn, flowers, vegetables and fruit trees. Even before the Woolfs moved to Monk's House, Virginia wrote of her husband as 'a fanatical lover' of the garden. As a young Cambridge student, Leonard holidayed in Cornwall and fantasised about chucking in scholarship for life as a day labourer. At their old rented country house Asheham, he gloried in 'potatoes ... broad beans, French beans, Japanese anemones, nasturtia, phlox & dahlias & a forest of weeds'. Taking a break from his Labour meetings, political research and publishing, he made jam, collected mushrooms and wildflowers, chopped wood and picked apples. With Virginia, he worked, gardened, then worked ('In the morning', wrote Leonard to Lytton Strachey, 'we write 750 words ... in the afternoon we dig').

'I'm always losing him in the garden', Virginia wrote of Leonard in a good-natured letter to Ethyl Smyth. 'He's up a tree, or behind a hedge.' From her letters, we see Leonard as an irrepressible, inexplicable saint of the secateurs—even in the most violent weather, or the most painful personal circumstances. In January of 1922, hail 'spat' in their fireplace, and gales tore the branches from trees. 'Leonard planted, pruned, sprayed', wrote his wife admiringly, 'though the cold & the wet & the wildness made his behaviour a heroism to be admired not comprehended'.

Almost twenty years after buying Monk's House, Leonard lost Virginia to her final madness, then suicide. The last words of her last diary entry were written on 24 March 1941: 'L. is doing the rhododendrons'.

In the grief-stricken years after Virginia's death, Leonard tended to the fruit trees, hedges and hothouse flowers, his sitting room decorated with yellow and double scarlet *Begonia*, lilies, *Gloxinia*. He added bee-hives, two greenhouses, and over six acres of land. One young novelist thought he chose brown flannel shirts because they didn't show dirt stains. He sent gingko seeds to an obsessive American fan. 'His long fingers seem faintly dusty', wrote Sussex author Diana Gardner, 'with chalky garden soil'. To Trekkie Parsons, his later love, he gave white *Freesia* and a red *Cyclamen*. In the year before he died, Leonard (and his new gardener) won a total of thirteen first prizes in the spring and summer horticul-tural shows of 1968. Just in case his works and awards left any doubt, the octogenarian listed his life's pleasures in the last volume of his autobiography, *The Journey Not the Arrival Matters*. Alongside friendships, food and sport, Leonard Woolf wrote 'cultivating a garden'.

The Pain of the World

Given his life-long passion for gardening, we might expect Woolf to have happy childhood recollections. Yet Leonard's earliest, and most disturbing, vision of the garden was one of sadness, alienation and what he called 'Weltschmerz': literally 'world pain'.

Before his father died, young Leonard lived with his family in a new house at 101 Lexham Gardens, London. It was a well-off, middle-class Victorian household, led by an absent but loving father and governed by a dreamy but practical mother. Barrister Sidney Woolf, like his son, was wiry, energetic and quick-witted. Marie Woolf was, Leonard reflected, soft, schoolgirlish and a little quirky. They were a happy, hard-working couple of decent, tolerant outlook. At the rear of their house, in a parallelogram of high brick walls and the back of the terrace, was a garden. There, with his eight siblings, little Leonard gardened in sooty London soil.

In the summers, Marie scouted then secured a holiday home, then the Woolfs' menagerie—'nine children, servants, dogs, cats, canaries and at one time two white rats in a bird-cage'—piled into an omnibus and a reserved railway carriage for their month or so out of Kensington.

After one vacation, when Leonard was perhaps five years old, he eagerly ran into the backyard. He was longing to see his flowers, bright amidst the filthy bricks. But to his horror, the colour and vitality had vanished. It was a scene of decay, death and a kind of vague, primal malice. Woolf's prose is that of an older man, looking back with the benefits of age and education. But his description of his childhood horror, inspired by Ecclesiastes, is striking:

> There the garden lay in its grimy solitude. There was not a breath of air. There were no flowers; a few spindly lilac bushes drooped in the beds. The grimy ivy drooped on the grimy walls. And all over the walls from ivy leaf to ivy leaf were large or small spider-webs, dozens and dozens of them, quite motionless, and motionless in the centre of each web sat a large or a small, a fat or a lean spider ... I can still smell the smell of sour earth and ivy; and suddenly my whole mind and

body seemed to be overwhelmed with melancholy ... I had experienced for the first time ... that sense of cosmic unhappiness which comes upon us when those that look out of the windows be darkened, when the daughters of music are laid low, the doors are shut in the street, the sound of the grinding is low, the grasshopper is a burden and desire fails.

In Lexham Gardens, Leonard Woolf's sadness was brought on not by this or that fact, but by the world itself: the way all things are destroyed, or simply crumble; the way strife quickly replaces harmony, and death life—the ivy grows, the spiders feed, the flowers wilt. For the young Woolf, the universe was a battleground between blind, irrational and ceaseless forces—not a

divine miracle, but a vain struggle. This is what, in 'The Gentleness of Nature', Woolf described as nature's 'ruthless ferocity, her dark and gloomy ways'.

As Leonard saw it, this savagery has no grand purpose, rationale or significance. While he was devoted to the pursuit of truth, Woolf knew absolute, perfect knowledge was impossible. Men are fallible and partial. Their ideals and impulses ultimately have no significance. 'I feel profoundly in the depths of my being', he wrote in *Sowing*, 'that in the last resort, *nothing matters*'. And he gave this harsh yet liberating advice throughout his life to friends and colleagues, often in heavy capitals.

Of course, a great many things 'mattered' to Leonard Woolf—including 'cultivating a garden'. He was undoubtedly a restrained, disciplined man, but he loved and wept and raged like anyone else. His love letters to Virginia were tender and gushing—they had nicknames for one another (he was 'Mongoose', she 'Mandril'). He once pulled his thumb out of joint, dreaming of strangling a man, and planned to 'work all morning and engage a whore for the afternoon' in Ceylon. Woolf never stopped loving, studying, writing, lobbying, conversing, publishing or caring for his sick wife. We owe the League of Nations, the precursor to the United Nations, partly to a man whose motto was 'NOTHING MATTERS'.

Leonard's point in *Sowing* and elsewhere was existentialist, not nihilistic; while he respected the historical figure of Jesus Christ (and would've published his Sermon on the Mount, he said), Woolf's was a godless universe. And unlike some of his peers, Woolf didn't replace religion with the easy certainties of nationalism, patriotism, fascism or Soviet communism. He thought these absolute, rigid herd movements had dismantled the best of civilisation; had made happiness, in politics, a 'dirty word'.

Leonard believed that, in spite of our strong passions and ideals, it is all up for grabs. No creeds or faiths can hide the gulf between hope and reality. Most of what we do, argued Woolf, in the chase for what excites or inspires us, is pointless and fruitless (in his lifetime, Leonard estimated he had endured 'between 150,000 and 200,000 hours of perfectly useless work'). Woolf had the courage to see the beauty in the world, but also the futility of it all: we strive and love, but the cosmos is a vast, dumb play of forces, without any ultimate plan or purpose.

Woolf kept up his existentialist credo until the end of his life. In fact, by the time he met Virginia, his opinions on nature had intensified, and come to include our inner lives, which he understood as chronically frail or savage. Much of this attitude was informed by his career in colonial Ceylon, now Sri Lanka—a more basic education in nature's 'dark and gloomy ways'.

The Jungle

Leonard's almost seven years in Sri Lanka reaffirmed the grim lesson of Lexham Gardens, and deepened its influence on the young Englishman. Having failed to cram for his Cambridge and Civil Service examinations, Woolf was offered low-level domestic jobs. But his marks were good enough to choose a higher post in the colonies. So on 19 November 1904, aged almost twenty-four, Leonard Woof set sail for the Subcontinent. It was absolutely alien to him—the heat, the stench, the flies, the primitive lifestyle and the atmosphere of baked melancholy (Leonard's letters are riddled with the word). 'It seems ridiculously a dream to me', he wrote five hours into the capital, Colombo. Like many Britons, he was often sick: he suffered dysentery, painful nausea, heatstroke and chronic eczema. He was disgusted by the insects: as he wrote one letter, he had two cockroaches climbing up his leg, a cricket down his back, a 'minor plague' of mosquitoes and flies, and a 'huge flying beetle' fly into his eye. His dog, Charles, soon died from the climate and food. This was Leonard's second birth—his new, bewildering, foreign life.

As characterised in letters to Lytton Strachey, Leonard's early days were marred by banality, sadness and poor company. For years he contemplated suicide. He was, he said, 'stunned by the madness and bitterness of life'. He worried that he'd never laugh again. To avoid boredom and illness, he kept himself busy with racquetball, squash, tennis and hockey, and mocking the expatriates ('The women', he wrote to Strachey, 'are all whores or hags or missionaries or all three'). Despite his colonial attitude, Woolf eventually grew to love the Ceylonese and the landscape—he enjoyed talking Sinhalese with the Buddhists, and exploring their Eastern philosophy; he hunted, bicycled and spent many hours in the overwhelming, brutal solitude of the jungle. He indulged his love for animals—a simple, pure affection.

But above all, Leonard laboured. He was uncomfortable with the power relations between the British and the Ceylonese, and recognised the limits of the law. But Woolf believed that the best way to reform the law was to apply it vigorously; to demonstrate its shortcomings in practice, rather than avoiding them illegally. The result was a strange combination of diligence and doubt. At first he counted pennies, checked accounts, signed letters, oversaw local disputes. Later promoted, he was in charge of Hambantota, a district in southeast Ceylon, and presided unwillingly over hangings. 'I work, God how I work', he wrote to Lytton Strachey in late 1908, when he was promoted to assistant government agent. 'I have reduced it to a method and exalted it to a mania.' In *Growing*, the second volume of his autobiography, he wrote of his love for efficiency—he always chased 'the most economical, quickest ... the most methodical'. As an administrator and magistrate, he applied laws, however unjust, with force and consistency. It left Leonard disliked by the English and Ceylonese alike—he was one of the 'evils' brought by Halley's comet, according to the locals. Still, Woolf pressed on, seeking order and precision—he believed in the law, regardless of his doubts about colonial rule. And he was rewarded for this, with promotion and greater authority.

But Woolf's administrative strictness concealed a greater scepticism about British rule. For him, the colonial order was precarious and held no dominion over the jungle ('a land of blood and mange'). In his indifferent, violent cosmos, nothing lasted—all civilised achievements were fragile, and ultimately lost. This was also, for Woolf, true of the mind: happiness and sanity are temporary achievements at best. It was an insight compounded by his later marriage to Virginia.

An arresting example of this was given in Woolf's novel *The Village in the Jungle*, which he wrote after his return to England in 1911. Praised by British administrators and Ceylonese citizens for its fidelity to peasant life, Leonard's novel has been in print in Sri Lanka since it was published.

The book reveals a cast of mind conditioned by the colonial preoccupation with civilisation. Written through the eyes of the Sinhalese villagers—rather than the British colonials, or Tamils—it tells the story of a single village, Beddagama, in the jungle of Ceylon. Woolf refuses to romanticise the jungle's wildness. It is a 'great sea' of stunted, drought-ravaged trees, with waves of hot wind. Leafless trees ooze white sap, and stringy lichen hangs on branches. The dying, dry ocean is deep with thorns, which cover the sterile dirt and sand. 'All jungles are evil', he wrote, 'but no jungle is more evil than that which lay about the village of Beddagama'.

Trying to survive in this village is Silindu, a weak-minded man, with two beautiful daughters: Punchi Menika and Hinnihami. He labours, kills animals, forages, but is always in debt to the headman. Amidst the 'living wall' of the jungle, the uneducated, unskilled villagers like Silindu are helpless—the headman and his clique are always in credit: thieving money, food and women. Like the beasts of the jungle, their lusts and hungers are satisfied by preying on fellow villagers. When Punchi Menika and Hinnihami refuse to be sexual chattels, they and their father are brutally, coolly manipulated. The story has the inevitability of Greek tragedy: in the end, three villagers are murdered; two are imprisoned, and the rest flee their huts. Only one, Punchi Menika, remains, alone, as the jungle slowly reclaims the village. Woolf's description is a plaintive, unsettling passage:

> The jungle moved within the walls: at last they crumbled; the tiled roof fell in. The grass and the weeds grew up over the little mound of broken red pottery; the jungle sticks of the walls spread out into thick bushes. Tall saplings of larger trees began to show themselves. By the end of the third rains the compound and the house had been blotted out.

The author's point is unambiguous: decay and destruction are always waiting to take over, for mankind to slip, grow selfish and upset the fragile balance of society. The jungle is first within, then without—first man's greed, or vanity, then the 'impenetrable disorder of thorns and creepers' as civilisation recedes.

Marriage and War

Leonard took this message home with him to England in 1911 when he returned from the service. Not long after, he married Virginia Stephens, the daughter of the then well-known literary critic Leslie Stephens. Virginia was from a rich, well-connected family, and combined the confidence and conceit of privilege with intense physical and social awkwardness. Not as classically beautiful as her sister Vanessa, Virginia nonetheless made a striking impression on the young man, just back from the colonies. He called her 'Aspasia', after Pericles' smart, educated mistress ('I am in love with Aspasia and have … flung myself at her feet'). The feeling, happily, was mutual, albeit with more caution on Virginia's part. Virginia was not sure what to make of this 'penniless Jew', as she called him, but she certainly flirted with him, in her clumsy way. 'Her method of wooing is to talk about nothing but fucking', wrote her brother Adrian, 'which she calls with a great leer copulation and WCs and I dare say she will be successful'.

By the time Woolf was settled in London, Virginia and Vanessa had moved into Brunswick Square, which became the headquarters for what was eventually known as 'Bloomsbury'. Leonard visited Brunswick Square regularly and spent what he called 'the most exciting months of my life' with Virginia. They candidly discussed books, art and politics, but also marriage. With characteristic frankness, they spoke about their own personal defects, their friends' affairs and indiscretions, and their hopes for children. The next year, in August 1912, they were married.

The Woolfs had a loving, tender and very productive marriage, albeit a childless one. They were both hardworking, dedicated to the written word and fond of blunt, witty conversation. As their Monk's House writing regimes suggest, they gave one another space to work and socialise, without ever sacrificing their own daily intimacies. But Virginia was ill—violently, worryingly, regularly. It began with headaches and general weakness, and soon progressed to anorexia, hallucinations and physical aggression. Within a few years of their wedding, Virginia had already attempted suicide once, swallowing an overdose of Veronal. She spent months recuperating at her brother George's Sussex country house, Dalingridge Place. Her weight dropped alarmingly; she attacked nurses, and she required constant supervision—often by Leonard.

While Woolf was a dutiful carer and administrator—scheduling her meals, social calls, work routines—these episodes took their toll on him. He also lost weight. He also suffered acute headaches. He kept at it because he loved Virginia and desperately wanted the return of normality. But it confirmed his outlook: the world could not be expected to be constantly safe or harmonious; it had to be controlled, diligently and stoically. In a letter to Clive Bell, Lytton Strachey observed that Leonard offered 'not a word of complaint and not the dimmest sign of snottishness from start to finish'. He speculated that this was 'Jewish training', and Leonard later agreed in his memoirs. But it was also the discipline born of Leonard's Ceylon service, and the outgrowth of his childhood attitude. For Woolf, sanity was only ever a temporary state—some were just more successful than others at maintaining it. There was no stigma, no horrified recoil; it was simply something to be conscientiously managed. Virginia's symptoms, he explained in *Beginning Again*, 'differed from the ordinary person's symptoms in degree rather than in kind'. Without sleep, good food and exercise, anyone could move from normality to exhaustion to madness. 'Everyone', he continued with his usual bluntness, 'is slightly and incipiently insane'.

Woolf viewed World War I, which began two years after their marriage, with a similar combination of dread and pragmatism. For him, the Great War destroyed much of rural England: not only its rolling landscape, lost to acre plots filled with 'bungalows, houses, shops, shacks, chicken runs, huts, and dog kennels', but also the rhythms and values of country life. Woolf's Sussex was not bombed, of course—that happened a generation later. Instead, it was sold for postwar reconstruction projects, making livelihoods and homes for servicemen, and keeping the economy kicking over. More horrifically, there were the casualties: Leonard's brother Cecil was killed by a German shell, and another brother, Philip, was severely wounded—two of the thirty-five million soldiers dead or wounded by the end of the war. The impression from Woolf is one of extraordinary waste—the end of Victorian England, and the beginning of a more alienated, accelerated age. Typically, Woolf did not dedicate long passages to lamentations, but simply reflected on the wasted opportunity. 'I don't see the point in destroying', he wrote in *Beginning Again*, 'unless you put something rather better in the place of what you destroy'. The war hit his generation, said Woolf, as a 'bolt from the blue', which belied the slow spread of civilisation they had expected. But with hindsight, he saw that the forces involved in the modern conflicts were always present in the human psyche and society. The great achievement he perceived in Western civilisation—the development and protection of precious individuality, the 'I'—was contingent and frag- ile. The forces that destroyed this 'I', Woolf argued in *The Journey Not the Arrival Matters*, could not always be stopped; they could only be managed or delayed—hence Woolf's work, during and after the war, on the League of Nations. His political labours gave no guarantees of peace and progress, but they helped to stem the tide of violence and barbarism for a little while longer.

This outlook remained for Woolf as World War II loomed. His friends Lytton Strachey and Roger Fry died, then his nephew Julian Bell was killed while driving an ambulance in the Spanish Civil War. Woolf's mother also died. While they were not especially close, Leonard none- theless felt her absence keenly. 'As the coffin is lowered into the grave', he wrote in *Downhill All the Way*, 'there is a second severance of the umbilical cord'. These losses helped to set the morbid scene for World War II, which seemed inevitable to Woolf—he could only watch 'help- lessly and hopelessly' its approach. While this modern war was unique in its mechanical savagery, the seem- ingly unstoppable turn to mass slaughter was something common to all ages of history. 'From the beginning of history, men and women ... have always faced the great crises and disasters, the senseless and inexorable results of communal savagery and stupidity', he wrote, 'with the calm, grim, fatalistic resignation of ... all of us in Rodmell and London in August and September 1939'.

Virginia killed herself in 1941, before the war ended. She had become increasingly depressed, her mental state an unfortunate consequence of stress and overwork, having just finished her last book, *Between the Acts*. Her diary entries were erratic and sometimes morbid. 'Are these the things that are interesting?' she wrote in January, 'that recall: that say Stop, you are so fair? Well, all life is so fair at my age ... And t'other side of the hill there'll be no rosy blue red snow'. The headaches, sleeplessness and hallucinations returned, terrifying her. Leonard recognised the signs of 'incipient' insanity early on and tried to manage the illness. 'The only chance for her', he wrote, 'was to give in and admit that she was ill, but this she could not do'.

Unsurprisingly, given his life and marriage, Leonard's cosmology was a bleak one: it was a small step, for Woolf, from Ceylon's mad buffalo and creepers to Virginia's madness and war—both were nightmares, he wrote in *Beginning Again*, only one was private, the other public. In each case, life was a continual struggle with the jungle.

This philosophy is hardly the halcyon dream of an English cottage garden, where wildness is a colourful impression, not a threatening fact. Pursued by this vision, it's a wonder Woolf did not flee to the sterile safety of a city flat, its bricks and stone untroubled by fractious life. As we know, he did not. Unlike his fellow Londoners, he preferred the country. The garden and Sussex landscape entranced him. At first blush, this seems a contradiction. For all his recognition of the garden's horror and decay,

Leonard Woolf spent a lifetime in amongst the dirt, worms and storms, getting his hands filthy.

He certainly did not expect to find immortality in his garden. Virginia once called him inside to hear Hitler's speech on the wireless. 'I shan't come. I am planting iris reticulata', he said, 'and they will be flowering long after he is dead' (as Leonard noted in *Downhill All the Way*, they *were*). But this small measure of longevity could not undo the forces of nature, and Woolf knew this. 'I take no interest', he wrote in the final volume of his memoirs, 'in the little odds and ends of me—my books, the Press, my garden, my memory—which might persist for a few years after my death'. The garden offered no consolation for mortality. But it was a striking symbol of grim defiance: pressing on with life, despite its futility. 'I looked upon work', he wrote, 'as a natural function or even a law of nature'.

Woolf was also using the garden as a retreat from people—'rank stupidity and uncharitableness', as he put it in *Beginning Again*. 'For a few moments one had succeeded in getting oneself out of the world of one's fellow man', he wrote in *Growing*, 'which I always do with a sigh of relief'.

Flowers and Ashes

But Woolf was doing more in the garden at Monk's House than simply soldiering on, or avoiding the traps of society. His embrace of gardening was a philosophical commitment. Specifically, he was confronting profound conflicts in the world and within himself. Throughout Woolf's writings there is a tension between order and disorder, which revealed itself in various forms: law versus anarchy, rational thought versus irrational faith, peace versus violence, sanity versus madness. In each case, Leonard was ostensibly on the side of the former. It was a vision of security, reason, precision, righteousness and psychological balance—however precarious—that endured over his long life. In *The Journey Not the Arrival Matters* he summed it up as the justice and mercy of the Hebrews and the liberty and beauty of the Greeks. This passage from *Sowing* makes the point keenly, lamenting the loss of his childhood security:

> Though in the course of my life I have passed through several desolations of desolation more desolate than the garden with its grimy ivy and its spider webs, I never again found any safety and civilization to equal that of the gas-lit nursery.

This battle was played out within Woolf's own psyche. 'To be even a moderately civilized man', he wrote in *Downhill All the Way*, 'is not only difficult but painful'.

What singled out Leonard Woolf was his frankness about this. He recognised this fundamental conflict, acknowledged his power or helplessness, and kept on. Leonard was certainly a private man, despite his very public persona. He believed that his 'I' was precious, and it was a 'horrible, an uncivilized thing' to drown it. For Woolf, the home was where this 'I' was safeguarded. The garden, in particular, was one of his chosen asylums from public life, and perhaps from Virginia's psychological volatility. But because of his honesty, Monk's House never became a flight from truth. Instead, the garden provided him with an image of unavoidable conflict—in the world, and within his own psyche. It echoed all his public and existential struggles. He could simultaneously enjoy his taste for rigor and precision, while recognising the principles of decay, violence and corruption. His Sussex garden was the 'cruel and dangerous' jungle of Ceylon, and the order of the colonial offices. It was wartime anxiety and pent-up domestic lust, but also moments of hard-won literary or marital contentment. It was decay and growth, death and rebirth.

In this regard, Monk's House was vital after Virginia's suicide. For weeks after he discovered her note, Leonard was numb, sometimes paralysed. 'I was like some hunted animal', he wrote in *The Journey Not the Arrival Matters*, 'which exhausted can only instinctively drag itself into its hole or lair'. But he still had his characteristic industry. He penned articles, published at Hogarth Press, edited the *New Statesman* and *Political Quarterly*, and kept a hand in the Fabian Society and Labour Party. And, not surprisingly, he gardened. Within a month of Virginia's death, their office apartment in Mecklenburgh Square was again bombed. Still grieving, Leonard drove to London, but quickly returned home to garden. The next day, teenagers bicycling and playing by the Ouse found Virginia's body in the water, three weeks after her suicide. He identified her at the mortuary—*and then gardened the next day*. His diary, written in smudged green ink, reads: 'Work Drove Newhaven inquest Garden'. Woolf had Virginia cremated, and buried her ashes in the great lawn, at the foot of an elm tree—one of two, named Leonard and Virginia. Each time he walked on that grass, or heard the elm's familiar shush, Woolf was no doubt painfully aware of his loss. After the war, when Leonard 'cultivated ... gardens passionately' with his new companion, Trekkie Parsons, he did so with Virginia's memory nearby. In his final decade, he often tended to his orchard, including Mr Prothero, an apple tree he and his wife had named at Monk's House fifty years earlier. In his memoirs, he called this Fate—not some mystical pre-destination, but the accumulated force of history, public and private. There was no point trying to escape this. He could only accustom himself to it stoically, with 'silent, unyielding self-control'.

This was why Leonard Woolf, middle-aged man of letters, donned two pairs of socks and pruned apples in Sussex's frozen January. The garden was his personal struggle with a conflicted but beloved cosmos. It would not last, and neither would he. But it was worth holding onto, for precisely the reason books were worth reading and writing: a clearer, saner, more honest life. With his dirty hands and chilled bones, Leonard was confronting life's basic ambivalence—one apple tree at a time.

Friedrich Nietzsche: The Thought-Tree

Whatever in nature ... is of my own kind, speaks to me, spurs me on, and comforts me; the rest I do not hear or forget right away. We are always only in our own company.

Friedrich Nietzsche, *The Gay Science*

Friedrich Nietzsche loitered under a lemon tree, muttering to himself. To the locals of Sorrento, the orchard was nothing special: a source of fruit and Limoncello, their famous bittersweet liqueur. But for the young philosopher—then thirty-three, on leave from his Basel professorship—the citrus grove was much more. Shading his red, squinting eyes from Italy's autumn sun, Nietzsche walked and collected his 'wicked thoughts'. It was a vital part of his daily philosophical routine.

For the delicate Prussian-born author, the morning began with warm milk and a cup of tea. Then there was dictation of letters or ideas to Albert Brenner, another young German staying at the Villa Rubinacci, which was rented by their patron Malwida von Meysenbug. Then Nietzsche took himself off for a long walk—often for hours. His ideas came as he strolled, or wandered under the foliage. And they came copiously. In her memoirs, Meysenbug described Nietzsche's furious work as he tried to finish his new book before madness and death stole him away (he lived another ten years before the first, and twenty before the second). Decades after that autumn, Meysenbug took the trouble to immortalise one detail: every time Nietzsche stood under this one particular tree, a thought 'fell' to him. His biographer Curtis Cate says this was called Nietzsche's *Gedankenbaum*, or 'thought-tree'.

Throughout his career, Nietzsche did much of his thinking in gardens, parks and woods. 'I need a blue sky above me', he told his friend Paul Deussen, 'if I am able to collect my thoughts'. For this reason, Nietzsche was very particular about his homes: they needed just the right combination of landscape and climate. In Nice, in early 1887, he saw forty houses before finally choosing. And once settled, he rarely stayed for long. His yearly itinerary was a continual, vain chase for the perfect weather. When he was pensioned off by Switzerland's Basel University in May 1879, he fled to Davos in the mountains. But the weather was not promising, so he moved to St Moritz, in the Engadine mountains. 'It is as if I was in the Promised Land', he wrote buoyantly to his sister Elizabeth. But his new Eden was soon mired in cloud and snow. So he headed to Venice, Marienbad in Bohemia, Naumburg in Germany, Basel, then several more Italian towns. 'Where is the land with a lot of shade', he asked his friend, the composer Henrich Köselitz, 'an eternally blue sky, and equally strong sea-wind from morning till evening, without thunderstorm?' Nietzsche died having never discovered his utopia.

One reason for Nietzsche's fussiness about where he lived was illness. In 1876, before his departure for Italy, Nietzsche was diagnosed with blindness and prescribed deadly-nightshade eye drops. In agony, he rationed his reading to an hour or so a day—a pittance for a scholar like Nietzsche. This is partly why he craved the lemon tree's shade in Sorrento: to stave off eyestrain and crippling headaches from the Italian sun.

Another reason was that Nietzsche was a loner of sorts, easily bruised by praise and condemnation. When *Human, All Too Human* was published in 1879, Nietzsche was struck with nausea and vomiting—a psychosomatic ailment, caused by the knowledge that his book was being read. His relations with women also swung between abandon and depression, as he gave himself over to the fantasy of love or marriage, and was then crushed by reality. After his disastrous, abortive *ménages* with Paul Rée and Lou Salomé, Nietzsche was so ill he was ready to shoot himself. Of course the philosopher could be witty, amiable and charismatic at times. But Nietzsche was not made for ongoing intimacy. For this reason, he craved solitude. 'That I would be alone by the time I was about forty— about this', he wrote to Köselitz in April 1884, after the Salomé affair, 'I have never had any illusions'. For Nietzsche's hero, the eponymous Zarathustra, the alpine forests were an escape from 'parasites, bogs, vapours'— metaphors for what he saw in the towns. Herr Professor Nietzsche was little different. 'We like to be out in nature so much', he wrote in *Human, All Too Human*, 'because it has no opinion of us'. Italy's lemon grove was, for the philosopher, comfortingly inhuman—a little *Lebensraum*, 'living space', or what he called, in *Beyond Good and Evil*, 'the "good" solitude'.

Walking in Ourselves

In the landscape, the philosopher was also seeking *himself*: a 'higher' Nietzsche, who was best discovered in groves or on mountainsides, rather than in churches or seminar rooms. In *The Gay Science* he said that his ideal building needed cloisters, so he could be closer to rocks, flowers and trees, and thereby closer to himself. 'We wish to see ourselves translated into stone and plants,' wrote Nietzsche, 'we want to take walks *in* ourselves, when we stroll around these buildings and gardens'. This was partly a criticism of religious architecture, with its Christian symbolism—oppressive for the atheist. But it was also because nature reminded him of his own existential ambitions.

This project hinged on Nietzsche's radical philosophy of nature, and his criticisms of nineteenth-century thought. The intellectual mood at the time was broadly idealistic. While science was growing rapidly, many scientists— including Darwin—were still deists who believed that the mechanical universe had a supernatural inventor. In philosophy, many of the ruling theories were Christian, or inspired by traditions sympathetic to Christianity, like Platonism. Another popular movement was Romanticism—a broad artistic church, which often saw emotion, spontaneity and organism as fundamental. Common to both traditions was the conviction that nature, broadly understood, had some special value or purpose, intelligible to the theologian, prophet or artist.

Nietzsche—the pious son of a pastor, and a devoted follower of Wagner and other Romantic composers— was originally moved by both traditions. But he eventually saw his era as self-deceiving, mistakenly giving nature human characteristics, like rationality or feeling, and revelling in sentimentality instead of brutal honesty. Seeing the world as 'lack of order, arrangement, form, beauty, wisdom, and whatever other names there are for our aesthetic anthropomorphisms', Nietzsche had no truck with nature as an organism or machine, artwork or divine law—these were all deceptive metaphors. Most involved metaphysics: the idea of an intelligible world, which belied or justified the perceivable one. 'All that has produced metaphysical assumptions, and made them *valuable, horrible, pleasurable* to men thus far', he wrote in *Human, All Too Human*, which he was composing as he strolled in Sorrento, 'is passion, error, and self-deception'. A genuine thinker, for Nietzsche, was able to confront the universe as it was, without inventing some deity, spirit or grand destiny as a cosmological or existential guarantor.

But for Nietzsche, this philosophical maturity was rare. Because of this, enlightened Europe was haunted by nihilism—what he called, in *The Will to Power*, the 'uncanniest of all guests'. The growth of reason and science, Nietzsche argued, often went hand in hand with idealism and sentimentality. Think of Darwin's deist god, comforting the naturalist as he developed his 'godless' hypothesis: evolution by natural selection. But all over the West, progressively more of mankind and nature were deprived of supernatural explanation and validation. New disciplines arose, which applied empirical, logical analysis to more domains: psychology, anthropology, sociology, alongside the physical sciences (Nietzsche called himself a 'psychologist'). Traditional ideas—god, soul, divine grace, predestination—lost their taken-for-granted truth. For many, the result was nihilism: having invented and believed in eternal and universal ideals, modern man was disoriented and disillusioned without them. Without some religious or cosmic source of value, there *was* no value—or so it suddenly seemed. This is why, in *Thus Spoke Zarathustra*, Nietzsche boldly proclaimed the 'death of God': not because there ever was a god, or because the philosopher was a deicide, but because the West was slowly destroying its own illusory footholds—and was struck by profound vertigo as it did so. This was the point of the madman's marketplace harangue in *The Gay Science*:

Is there still any up or down, are we not straying as through an infinite nothing, do we not feel the breath of empty space, has it not become colder, is not night continually closing in on us ... do we hear nothing as yet of the noise of the grave diggers who are burying God? Do we smell nothing as yet of the divine decomposition?

Contrary to his reputation, Nietzsche's response to this divine funeral was not to champion nihilism—far from it. Instead, he believed the best minds had to be more honest about what they were doing all along: imposing themselves upon the world, and one another. He railed against the myth of 'pure' motives in art and scholarship. Importantly, Nietzsche had no moral problem with this; he simply wanted more candour and judiciousness. This is Nietzsche's famous doctrine of the 'will to power': mankind as just another selfish organism, at its best with physical strength, intellectual clarity and courage, emotional abundance. In this vision, we cannot look to the universe for ultimate value or ideas, or to society, but only to ourselves. 'What? A great man?' he asked in *Beyond Good and Evil*: 'I always see only an actor of his own ideal'. Greatness is a performance, in which we are the actors, audience and judges.

Free Spirits

For this reason, Nietzsche's cosmology stressed *process* above all: creation and destruction, growth and decay, birth and death. For Nietzsche, nature provided no 'should' or 'ought'. It was amoral. Its virtue was its fickleness and fertility. Animals and plants lived and died, but nature as a whole kept experimenting with new species and environments. It was a lesson in the brutality of evolution. But it also taught a certain profligacy: over millions of years, nature had been guiltlessly throwing away life for innovation's sake. There was no progress, no purpose, just a parade of novelty, which sometimes delivered beauty, strength and health—and sometimes disfigurement, impotence and disease.

Nietzsche's existential vision echoed this process. What he wanted of his supermen—Zarathustra, Dionysus, 'great man', 'free spirits'—was what he asked of himself: a willingness to guiltlessly destroy old ideas and values, regardless of the pain involved. To be honest, in other words, about human responsibility for human development, rather than deferring to a fictional ideal. And behind this was a strong will: able to bear pain, loneliness, mockery, grief, without giving up in favour of supernatural consolation. 'Philosophising with a hammer', he called it in *Twilight of the Idols*. Nietzsche's mallet-wielding *Übermensch* ('superman') was not just a destroyer, however. He believed in discipline, restraint, delicacy and subtlety. Nature taught Nietzsche how much of his psyche was organic and instinctual, but he mastered these with what, in *The Gay Science*, he called 'style'. 'Weak characters without power over themselves', he wrote, '*hate* the constraint of style'. Strong characters like Nietzsche willed themselves into existence in this way—even when they were lonely and ill, as was the philosopher.

In this new outlook, nature supplied the materials and tools, but not the blueprint: science, metaphysics or theology gave no certainties. Hence Nietzsche's contempt for anti-Semitism and nationalism, with their false foundations of biology or state, and his disgust with his own proto-Nazi brother-in-law, fooled by absurd notions of German superiority. They were not really supermen: they were weak fools, he believed, unwilling or unable to live without illusory certainty. Mankind, asserted Nietzsche, had to be *stronger*: to experiment with itself, without guarantees or promises—just like plants and animals. Nietzsche's supermen had to live dangerously and build houses next to Vesuvius, as he quipped in *The Gay Science*. They had to be like a tree on a cliff, he wrote in *Zarathustra*: 'calmly and attentively it leans out over the sea' (note the botanical metaphor for solitude and superiority). More literally, Nietzsche's great men had to forgo universities and salons, and get out into the earth's power and profligacy. Sitting thinking indoors was for 'nihilists' (he accused the French novelist Gustave Flaubert of this).

For Nietzsche, Sorrento's citrus grove offered no comforting vision of a lawful, benign cosmos—no relaxing break. It was a challenge to experiment: with his ideas, values, career and relationships. The 'thought-tree' asked him to turf the reassuring certainties of family, class and his traditional education; to be as violent, unpredictable and innovative as nature. In this way, Nietzsche's gardens helped him to press on with his radical innovations in theory, literature and the German language.

The result was decisive. Not long after Sorrento, Nietzsche's life was transformed. Significantly, he broke with his idol, the composer Richard Wagner, partly because of Wagner's overbearing attitude—curt letters ordering the young professor to send him pants did not sit well with Nietzsche's headaches and nausea. But it was also a philosophical separation. With his new-found naturalism, Nietzsche found Wagner too mystical, otherworldly, sentimental—too 'Christian', in a word. He also saw Wagner's increasing 'guru' status as a barrier to the composer's greatness. Too much fawning was robbing Wagner of proper criticism and opposition; the strife that drives great souls was replaced with sycophancy. In Wagner he saw decadent retreat. For similar reasons, Nietzsche also took issue with Arthur Schopenhauer, whose works he had lauded as a student. While respecting the German philosopher's steely pessimism, 'process' outlook and lively prose, Nietzsche accused him of Wagner's crime: a quietist, defeated withdrawal from the world. This was a life-denying philosophy, whereas the young philosopher wanted to say 'yes': to instinct, flesh and their natural foundations. The Nietzsche of Sorrento was increasingly an evolutionary advocate.

Nietzsche was also, after the Villa Rubinacci, increasingly alone. Coinciding with his increased naturalism was a greater urge to escape Basel's intellectual climate in favour of the seaside, alpine walks or occasional 'cures' abroad. He avoided big cities, parties and, after he received his pension from Basel University, academic employment. Gone was the urban classics scholar and Schopenhaurian Wagner disciple. In his place was a lone positivist philosopher, increasingly preferring the company of gardens and parks to books, cafes and professional peers. He would not have a conventional marriage, or—he soon realised—any marriage at all. He would become increasingly hostile to his mother's and sister's conservatism ('When I look for my profoundest opposite', he wrote in *Ecce Homo*, his autobiography, 'I always find my mother and my sister'). All this was bound up with his naturalistic bent and push to independence.

His eventual madness robbed him of this freedom; as he died in his sister's care, unaware of his own contribution to modern arts and letters, and his sister's Nazi perversion of it. But while he was lucid, Nietzsche achieved an impressive distance from conservative ideas, and distracting familial entanglements. The orchards and woods of Sorrento were a step in Nietzsche's path to becoming a radical philosopher. They encouraged the genius he stubbornly willed himself to become, even as his eyes and mind gave way.

In this way, the citruses helped Nietzsche to be the 'posthumous man' he proclaimed himself to be in *Ecce Homo*. In the decades after his death in 1900, Nietzsche's radical ideas had a profound influence on modern thought. Not as a single system, and much less the exalted spiritual authority co-opted by the Nazis, but as a legacy of intellectual courage, originality and clarity. 'What we are left with is not a doctrine that might be preached', as Nietzsche's biographer RJ Hollingdale put it, 'but a human individual, an artist in language of great skill and power, and a philosopher of compelling insight and strictness of principle'. Some of the greats of twentieth-century philosophy—Henri Bergson, Martin Heidegger, Michel Foucault, Jacques Derrida, to name a handful—owed Nietzsche an intellectual debt. Psychology, including the seminal works of Sigmund Freud and Carl Jung, has deep Nietzschean veins: the pathological conflict between individual and society; the unconscious and instinctual basis of art and ideas; the opacity of consciousness to itself. Nietzsche also informed artists and authors, from the epic modern novels of Thomas Mann and Robert Musil, to Mark Rothko's mythic colours and Giorgio de Chirico's still, surreal landscapes. The man whom biographer Rüdinger Safranski called a 'laboratory of thinking' still inspires the experiment of modern life and thought.

Become What You Are

A Nietzschean garden is a straightforward existential challenge. It is a lesson in Nietzsche's dictum, borrowed from the Greek poet Pindar: 'Become what you are'. Most obviously, nature offers an encounter with the planet's blind forces. The Nietzschean realisation that the cosmos is meaningless and pointless can be profoundly liberating. It suddenly makes common sense and traditional values look petty or small, which can be a vital first step toward the cultivation of independence. More importantly, it also suggests that second nature, *our* nature or *physis*, is unfinished; that humanity is not fixed by cosmological law or divine decree. This is Nietzsche's point: we are a work in progress, like Sorrento's lemons and firs—only we can craft ourselves more deliberately.

As a corrective, the garden also reveals how difficult this lived *Bildungsroman* is; how easily our freedom is compromised. However modern we are, we're still at the mercy of instinct, habit and reflex—as was Nietzsche with his strains of misogyny, for example. The garden mirrors this conflict: even the most pedantically clipped yard—mown, pruned and weeded—is continually subject to forces that override pattern and order. Yet Nietzsche believed our own nature can also be tamed. This is why, in *Human, All Too Human*, Nietzsche wrote of 'sobriety of feeling': we have to be somewhat ruthless with ourselves, to overcome addictions, delusions and false idols. The point is not abstract knowledge, but what the philosopher called 'style': a more striking, graceful and refined life, which boldly combines biological inevitability with psychological autonomy. And this is precisely the balance he saw in Sorrento, his childhood home in Röcken, and the roses and geraniums of Nice ('Not at all Nordic!' he noted mischievously to his sister and her husband). In his example and in the gardens that inspired it, Nietzsche challenges us to cultivate ourselves with courage and artistry, rather than giving in to distraction, or what's 'done'. 'How we hasten to give our heart to the state, to money-making, to sociability or science', wrote Nietzsche in 'Schopenhauer as Educator', 'merely so as no longer to possess it ourselves'.

The Wanderer

A decade after Sorrento's thought-tree, aged forty-four, Nietzsche went mad—perhaps from syphilis, contracted in one of his rare sexual encounters. But the landscape kept its existential value for him. While writing *Ecce Homo*, Nietzsche went into raptures over Turin's autumn. In October 1888 the philosopher wrote somewhat manically of the 'glorious foliage in glowing yellow', and 'the sky and the big river delicately blue'. Intellectual clarity was replaced by a kind of mythic luminosity—more prophetic than philosophical. 'A Claude Lorraine', he wrote of the city, referring to the French neoclassical landscape painter, 'such as I never dreamed'. Within months, he was signing his name 'Dionysus', and writing of his plans to shoot the Kaiser. In his poor, cracked psyche, Friedrich Nietzsche had finally become his superman, and all of Turin's gardens radiated with this tragedy.

Saddening as this is, it's important to see the lucidity of his lifelong devotion to gardens, and the outdoors.

Throughout his career, Nietzsche's unusual sensitivity to nature informed his ideas, symbolising a certain freshness and brightness of thought, free from metaphysical gloom and existential sloth. Nietzsche the mad, conspiratorial Dionysus was also Nietzsche the 'Wanderer' from *Human, All Too Human*, thankful for his thought-tree:

> He strolls quietly in the equilibrium of his forenoon soul, under trees from whose tops and leafy corners only good and bright things are thrown down to him, the gifts of all those free spirits who are at home in mountain, wood, and solitude, and who are, like him, in their sometimes merry, sometimes contemplative way, wanderers and philosophers.

Colette: Sex and Roses

I could gain my liberty at any moment by means of an easy climb over a gate, a wall, or a little sloping roof, but as soon as I landed back on the gravel of our own garden, illusion and faith returned to me.

Colette, *Sido*

Colette was modern France's most lauded woman author. But she also had a second career as a scandal. In 1893 she arrived in Paris from provincial Burgundy as the 20-year-old bride of an urbane cad, the writer Henry 'Willy' Gauthier-Villars. 'In a few hours an unscrupulous man', she wrote of her husband in *My Apprenticeships*, 'will transform an ignorant girl into a prodigy of licentiousness'. Colette had her literary apprenticeship as one of his ghostwriters before publishing her first novel, *Claudine at School*. The risqué tale, heavily edited by her husband, featured teenage promiscuity, lesbianism, teacher–student affairs and a casual disregard for bourgeois propriety. 'It promises something a bit more than glory to its author: *martyrdom*', said Rachilde in a review for the *Mercure de*

France, 'for there will never be enough stones or crowns of thorns to throw at her'.

Colette was undeterred, and continued to write best-selling Claudine novels in her 'little drawing-room jail', while Willy had his affairs. During their marriage, and after their strangely amicable divorce, Colette also performed raunchy pantomimes in a music hall to the applause of audiences and the consternation of establishment conservatives. She was a fashionable lesbian before it was fashionable. Her onstage kiss with her lover Mathilde (Missy) de Mourney, in a Moulin Rouge pantomime, caused such a fracas that the police were called. Still touring as an actress, Colette was also a journalist for *Le Matin*, a theatre critic, a novelist and a playwright— often under a pseudonym, because of her scandalous reputation.

Meanwhile, the drama continued in her life. After Missy and several other affairs with men and women, Colette married Henri de Jouvenel and had a child, also named Colette (nicknamed 'Bel-Gazou'), whom she gave to an English nanny to raise for most of the year. Polite society again raised its eyebrows when Colette seduced her teenage stepson Bertrand, some thirty years her junior. 'She belonged to the first generation', wrote Henri de Jouvenel's secretary, 'of twentieth-century sexual revolutionaries'. Ever the optimist, she went on to get married for a third time, to Maurice Goudeket. Throughout her life, Colette wrote prodigiously, keeping up what she called her 'merciless control' over prose, without putting the brakes on hedonism or notoriety. She also poured her funds, and those of rich (and perhaps credulous) friends, into 'Colette' branded beauty products ('Streetwalker' chic, according to one friend). Suffice it to say that, as a cosmetics entrepreneur, she was a fine author. Colette had no talent for this craft or industry, but she approached it with the same ferocity she did literature, sex, food and love. Colette could be cruel, fickle and deceitful. But in a conservative era, her chief scandal was her willingness, as a woman, to affirm her own ample appetites.

The Palais-Royal

More than four decades after Willy first showed her off to Paris, we find Colette still in the capital, in her new apartment in the Palais-Royal. She sits at her divan bed, a fur throw on her legs. Despite the pillows at her back, and her loose sandals, she is uncomfortable. Her back and hips ache. Her ankles and feet are swollen. And her hand, gripping the Parker Duofold, is bent with arthritis. Alongside her cats, her constant companion is, she says, 'pain ever young'. But her lamp, shaded with the famous blue paper, is on, so her friends know she is writing. More blue sheets sit on a card table on her lap's thick folds, alongside unread letters and a vase of fleshy pink roses. Her fountain pen glides quickly over the pages—'as easily as frying an egg', she once boasted. This Chevalier of the Legion of Honour is still on top of her literary game.

As she writes, she hears the Resistance snipers. 'The shots echoing and reechoing from wall to wall across the garden', she wrote in *The Evening Star*, 'provided a rather theatrical display'. Colette wants to lean on her windowsill to watch the shooting, but it is not safe ('they're such bad shots'). But in daylight, she savours the view.

Below are the neat geometries of the Jardin du Palais-Royal: eighteenth-century parterres around a dry fountain, bordered by avenues of lime trees. The sunlit mist of the morning has gone, and Colette's eyes flit between the paper's light blue and the greens outside her window. She sees the occupying German officers, pacing with their pistols holstered. She soaks up the Palais-Royal's rural idyll, right on her Paris doorstep—'another country home', as her friends put it. Scents of wisteria brought from her childhood home, bees landing on her window sill, and the noise of kids playing. She will die here, and the thought comforts her. 'I like the idea that I shall have to face my end', she writes in 'The Palais-Royal', 'watched over ... by the remains of an arbor that once gave shade to nuns'. She can almost smell the citrus leaves.

Almost. For Colette is bedridden. And as she ages, she will suffer this more regularly—already she must be carried downstairs to La Grand Vefour for her favourite salmon pastry. The room feels small, stuffy. The jardin's enlightenment lines are as far away as her old Saint-Tropez retreat, or the roses of her Burgundy childhood. No more training vines to climb iron arches, or staking tomatoes. Left hand gently stroking her wiry hedge of hair, she watches the window and writes. After a life of public notoriety, the septuagenarian author conjures up one of her last reveries: a garden.

'I don't have a garden any more', Colette writes in *Flowers and Fruit*. No matter—she will daydream. 'The worrying thing', she continues, 'would be if the future gardens, whose reality is of no importance, were beyond my grasp'. But her mind is still clear—the future can be written, if not lived. She'll plant blue *Hepaticas*, which will edge a basket of *Dielytras*. Her pansies, she says, will look like Henry VIII. She'll have an arbour and a trellis for dragon-tongued *Cobaeas*. Her vases will be stuffed with white lilies, and tuberose will climb the staircase. If it's a Breton garden, Colette will plant *Daphne*. If it's by a lake, she'll have Japan allspice—the nightingale of flowers, dull to look at but beautiful to other senses. 'How I love this ideal flower bed of mine', she writes, 'with its sumptuous border of "ifs"'. It's a grab bag of Colette's aesthetic passions, so practicality or feasibility are irrelevant. For her, the important thing is the fantasy itself—to ward off forgetfulness. 'I shall dig them all into their storage trenches, some in my memory, the others in my imagination', she writes. 'There ... they can still find the humus, the slightly bitter water, the warmth and the gratitude which will perhaps keep them from dying.' Because of her literary talent, Colette's fantasies seem palpable—as if the humus and bitter water were right by her day bed.

Virtuoso Playing

In her 'well-ordered solitude', Sidonie-Gabrielle Colette lived in two worlds, real and imagined. There was her Paris apartment, and its procession of entertainments: fan mail, cut flowers, visits from neighbour Jean Cocteau, with whom she traded barbs and closet-skeletons like 'precious marbles'. And there was her inner universe, her sumptuous border of 'ifs': two long roads of memory and fantasy, forking behind to childhood, and ahead to death and beyond. This tendency to daydream was more than a product of Colette's advancing age. If the years intensified her imagination, the disposition was always there. She loved the faded and the nascent with equal ferocity. This sounds schizoid, but it was not. Unifying all of Colette's flights was an ideal of tranquillity, centred on the French landscape, particularly flowers.

Most obviously, this stemmed from her bucolic child-hood at Rue de l'Hospice, in Saint-Sauveur-en-Puisaye, a Burgundy commune in the late nineteenth century. Her mother Sidonie—nicknamed Sido—was a keen green thumb, who shrugged off her domestic burdens in the fresh air. 'Off she would go', recalled Colette in *Sido*, 'into the garden, and at once her resentment and her nervous exasperation subsided'. All year round Sido guarded her 'babies': shelves of young potted plants, growing on green wooden steps. Colette once scratched into a pot's lifeless-looking dirt, trying to discover the bulb or seed. 'You're nothing but a little eight-year-old murder-ess', said her mother, angrily. Sido coveted her flowers, and was known to refuse roses for use in funerals, pel-argoniums for Corpus Christi. If she avoided state reli-gion, there was a secular reverence in this, which stamped itself upon Colette's soul. 'The style of things, the kind of things that we shall love in later life are fixed', she wrote in 'Autumn', 'in that moment when the child's strong gaze selects and molds the figures of fantasy that for it are going to last'. Daffodils ringing a spring, a family feast arranged like a bouquet, conifers dressed in snow—these provided Colette with her distinctive imagery. She took pleasure in them throughout her long life. They col-oured her prose, from her debut *Claudine at School* (her Sapphic teenager, Claudine, loves 'deep, encroaching woods') to her very last memoirs and essays.

Biographer Judith Thurman notes that happy child-hoods are 'as scarce in biography as they are in fiction'. She questions Colette's halcyon vision of girlhood, with its convenient contrast with urbane Parisian cynicism. But whatever their sources—fact or fiction, invention or revision—Colette's fantasies were consistent. Her works are full of intimate botanical and horticultural detail, often from her Burgundy childhood. 'I plunge off down a once familiar path at the pace I walked along it then', she wrote in *The Evening Star*. 'I aim for the big, crooked oak, for the poor farm where the cider and the bread spread with butter were doled out to me with such a generous hand.' If scenes like this were fictions, they were necessary ones for her. An insomniac, Colette spent whole nights this way, wandering in her past landscapes—what the author called her 'virtuoso playing upon memory'.

The imagined future had the same horticultural appeal. In 1925, when she was in her early fifties, Colette purchased a Saint-Tropez property. She did not buy it for the house, much less for the investment or cachet (it was then a place to buy seafood, not to be 'seen'). She bought it for the landscape, with its 4 acres of Mediterranean soil and flora. 'There is ... a house', she wrote, 'but that counts less'. She dubbed it 'La Treille Muscate': The Grape Vine. As soon as the house was hers, she began to invent her ideal garden. She painstakingly listed the tomatoes, aubergines, tarragon, sage, mint and yellow, pink and red roses. She devoted a purple paragraph to the vines, climbing iron arches and spiralling above the dirt. 'Already lyrical, already in ecstasy?' she chided herself, but then justified her fancy: 'The shores of the Mediterranean have turned more than one steady head with their intoxications'. Like many owners then and now, Colette was excitedly making plans for her new property. But this idea was more than a dry blueprint to be discarded in favour of the real thing. The idea *was* the real thing, to be played with in her mind. Hence her Bacchanalian prose, revelling in 'grapes with their taut-skinned curves ... wind laden with resins ... the yellow rose which has a scent of fine cigars'. This was a fantasy, enjoyed for its own sake.

The point is not that Colette was anaesthetised to the present. Even in her eighth decade she was still switched on. After a nervous visit in March 1948, Simone de Beauvoir told her American lover, Nelson Algren, that the ageing raconteur was so alive, 'nobody would think of looking at younger, finer women'. She was no doddering anachronism. The point is that, for Colette, the undone and unrealised—past and future, decay and renewal, recollection and invention—were equally real, and equally worthy of contemplation and joy. In her fantasies, she kept returning to visions of Breton soil, fleshy roses or grapevines. For Colette, this vision had a restorative, rejuvenating role.

Vital Insufficiency

In particular, the garden liberated Colette from her own appetites. As her no-holds-barred affairs suggest, Colette was motivated by particularly intense desires. But like many who've tasted abandon and transgression, she knew that the moments of joy never lasted. Hence the continual disappointment of her lovers in *The Pure and the Impure*: they were looking for respite from deprivation in one another, but deprivation was their fundamental condition. 'The lovers', summarises Thurman, 'give pleasure but can't receive it, or take it but can't give it, ... are mismatched in age, appetite, egotism, and experience—... all feel obscurely cheated'. This does not mean that pleasure did not exist for Colette—on the contrary, it could be an obsession, precisely because of its fleeting nature. There was still the frisson of sex with a much-younger stepson, or the straightforward pleasure of a rich salmon pie, or a cooling breeze on a sandaled foot. The point is that these gratifications were the exception, and not the rule. In Colette's mind, it led to a dog-eat-dog cosmos, in which all things were constantly craving something and usually competing with one another for it. 'How many crimes', said Colette in *Flowers and Fruit*, 'perpetrated by one kingdom upon another!' In Colette's world, craving never ended; one only discovered new things to crave, ad nauseam.

So for Colette, appetite was a central existential principle. It began with food: as a little girl with a fever, she pushed away medicinal chicken and rice pudding, and sighed: 'I'd like some Camembert, please'. After suffering violent food poisoning, she pigged out on stuffed cabbage, cider and a currant tart—the richer the meal, the better the rejuvenation. She was convinced that her friend Annie de Pene, who succumbed to the 1914 Spanish influenza epidemic, died because she had not eaten well. 'The flu took her with her defenses down', she wrote to a friend, 'which is to say on an empty stomach'. Hoping to remedy this by proxy, she tried to console Annie's daughter with a bunch of grapes, and then prawns at Prunier's. For Colette, food cured spiritual and bodily ills.

When she hit late adolescence and early youth, sex had the same restorative role—for one lover, at least. In *The Pure and the Impure*, Colette described this as if it were parasitism—lovers as vampires or victims. She wrote of 'individuals who let themselves be filled by me, leaving me empty and drawn'—like her bookish, teenage stepson, Bertrand de Jouvenel, whom she seduced in her fifties. In her youth, she was herself 'filled' by the rakish Willy. Colette was, she later wrote in *My Apprenticeships*, one of those 'barely nubile girls who dream of being the spectacle, the plaything, the erotic masterpiece of an older man'. For Colette, pleasure usually required some hierarchy: master and slave, domination and submission, predator and prey. 'I don't love people I can dominate', said her fifteen-year-old heroine Claudine, who wanted to be bullied a little by a lover. Even Colette's ties with pets and children were 'raptorial', as she put it—she had to 'conquer and subdue', lest they did the same to her. A child was, she wrote in *My Mother's House*, a 'happy little vampire'.

As this suggests, Colette played both roles, and excelled in each: the naïve nymphet with long braids, and the predatory seductress; the capricious, stubborn child, and the stern mother. At the heart of both was ongoing appetite: someone always needed to be 'fed', gastronomically, libidinally, psychologically. Because of this, Colette had an ongoing fear of emptiness: in herself, and the world. 'She utterly abhors a vacuum', writes Thurman, 'and her famous insatiability is proportional to her exaggerated terror of any vital insufficiency'. Hence Colette's distinctive hunger for Camembert, Bordeaux wine, transgressive love—all attempts to stave off some kind of physical or spiritual deprivation.

'Disinterested Botanical Passion'

The garden might seem an unlikely remedy for this exhausting appetite. After all, roses and truffles, just like French authors, are creatures of craving. They feed, procreate, die. Colette recognised this now and then, but rarely for long—plants were always given a 'get out of jail free' card. In *Prisons and Paradise*, for example, she reflected on flowers in light of modern science and cinema. Researchers suggested that plants had nervous systems, and therefore suffered pain, perhaps anxiety and anger. 'What! Are the flowers cruel too?' she wrote. 'Are they too the slaves of a demanding sexuality? Do they too have savage and cruel caprices?' Cinema portrayed plants on a gigantic scale, moving quickly with time-lapse photography. A climbing pea looked like a python, a lily like a crocodile. Colette was unsettled by these images, but she repressed her horror in favour of a rosier outlook. 'I would rather not know', she wrote in *Flowers and Fruit*, about a stinking carrion flower, surrounded by dying flies. 'Let the little black secret remain lying there in the depths of that flower-of-ill-repute.' Flowers, in Colette's world, had to stay pure. For her, they were an almost magical break from the normal laws of the universe. Hence the scenes in *Claudine at School*, with her town transformed into a flowery bower, a kind of youthful fantasy land.

This might seem like Jean-Paul Sartre's bad faith: recognising plants' voracious will with one breath, and denying it with another. And certainly Colette was not aiming at philosophical consistency in her life or writings. Perhaps this is why Sartre described her as a 'sacred monster', after dining with her: the normal rules of intellect and scholarship did not apply. Nonetheless, her love of flowers and gardens provided genuine respite from her private 'red in tooth and claw' universe. Whereas desire for sex or food always left Colette wanting more, plants helped to rid her of desire altogether; helped her to become less starved and more contemplative.

For Colette, there was nothing cryptic in flowers, nothing capricious or fickle. They did not lie, cheat, betray; they were what they were, in 1880 or 1932, in Paris or Burgundy. Put simply, flowers were straightforward: they had a common and continuous nature. Because of this, Colette felt she did not have to seduce or coerce them (and she fumed when urbanites blithely did so: 'Parisians nip all flowers in the bud', she grumbled). She was simply happy to observe nature's principles, what she called a 'labour which strives towards perfection'. More specifically, instead of seeing flowers as predators or prey, Colette considered them calmly. In *Prisons and Paradise*, she described this attitude as her 'disinterested botanical passion'. With this outlook, the flowers were no longer things to be measured and manipulated.

Each was a personality of sorts. Take her passage from *Prisons and Paradise*:

> Rose, increasing your dimensions, shrinking once more, perverted, disguised, and docile in the capricious hands of man, you still have the power, despite all this, to draw out from us, to *calm in us all that remains of love's old madness.*

Colette's rose was not just decoration. It was an invitation to imagine its distinctive character: what the German philosopher Arthur Schopenhauer called 'contemplation'. In this state, the contemplative consciousness 'ceases to consider the where, the when, the why, and the whither of things', wrote Schopenhauer, 'and looks simply and solely at the *what*'. With Colette, this was a kind of imaginative reconstruction. It began with recognition that flowers were not, like animals, particularly individuated—their personality transcended individual plants. Colette took their regular shapes, colours, rhythms, and transformed them into a kind of universal personality: what Schopenhauer called the 'one, unchanging Idea of the plant'. For example, pansies were like Henry VIII, 'common, but dignified ... self-satisfied ... quick to degenerate'. The anemone was decisive, biding its time then suddenly opening 'like a parachute seized by a gust of wind'. And roses had dynasties, with a hundred flowers like sisters in a single dynastic line ('Not quite different, not quite the same', she wrote). This is what Alain, in Colette's short story 'The Cat', loves in his mother's old garden: continuity, despite the years. 'Oh, the same, the very same salvias!' he cries, having left his young wife for his mother's garden. For Colette, this was not strictly scientific, but a kind of literary invention, which combined artistry with careful botanic observation. The aim was a less calculating, more generous, portrait of another life.

Toward the end, Colette's calm idealism grew more consistent. She wrote of the spirit of indifference in her relationships, for example. The 'pendulum swings of "give and take"' tired her, and she learnt to 'disport with equals', she said. This was partly because lust waned with age, but it was also because of the contemplative consciousness she displayed in the garden: a new distance, objectivity, restraint. Put another way, she did not seek out new lovers, novel dishes, rare vintages. Rather, she treated the old objects *differently*. She learnt to replace the 'little pink snout of love', as she once put it, with a less covetous gaze—a lesson partly gained from gardens in general, and flowers in particular. As with her mother, they freed Colette by training her to change her mode of consciousness.

This liberation was partial, to say the least. Thankfully for her readers, Colette never attained the dull, Buddhist-like resignation Schopenhauer recommended. She was too rapacious and vibrant to accept austerity, abstinence or isolation. Her writing was itself a kind of violent possession: skewering a character with the right word, phrase, metaphor, just like the butterflies pinned in her bedroom. Her manuscripts were riddled with crossings-out and corrections. 'There is a tired spirit deep inside of me', Colette said in *The Evening Star*, 'that still continues its gourmet's quest for a better word, and then for a better word still'. She kept at it, right until the end. Almost eighty, and drifting in and out of sociability and lucidity, she still struck Cocteau as a formidable presence. 'She comes into the bar, wheeled by the bartender', he wrote. 'I recognize her fine eyes swimming in the best Marennes oysters, her olive-tree hair, her mouth like an arrowhead wound.'

But alongside this vehemence was always Colette's idealism, her deep regard for the French landscape and its flora. Just after World War II, in her seventies, Colette published *The Evening Star*. In one of the more moving passages, the author imagined herself giving up writing altogether. Her companions in this fictional retirement? Neither her husband Maurice, nor her pinned butterflies, nor her crystal collection. Just flowers. 'I'm not at home to anyone', she imagined herself saying, 'except for this quadrangular forget-me-not, for this rose in the shape of a wishing well, for the silence in which the sound made by the mind when searching for the word has just died away'.

On 2 August 1954, aged eighty-one, Colette lay on her deathbed, leafing through an illustrated book on birds and butterflies. She was weak and quiet. Then suddenly she swept her hand over the book, and toward the window outside. 'Look', she said to her husband Maurice and housekeeper Pauline. 'Look!' They were Colette's last words.

Jean-Jacques Rousseau: Botanical Confessions

I am convinced that at any age the study of nature ...
bestows upon the mind a salutary nourishment
by filling it with a subject most worthy of its
contemplation.

> Jean-Jacques Rousseau, letter to Madame Étienne
> Delessert, 1771

Philosopher Jean-Jacques Rousseau's greatest talent was not logic, morality or metaphysics. It was self-portraiture. Rousseau's literary works left a striking sketch of the author: a new kind of eighteenth-century Frenchman, brave, sincere and just. This was idealised, of course. 'My innate goodwill towards my fellow men; my burning love for the great, the true, the beautiful', he boasted in his *Confessions*, 'my inability to hate, to hurt, or even to want to'. In the sentimental spirit of the age, and with more than a little conceit, Rousseau spared no superlatives when describing his own virtues.

Rousseau's literary persona inspired the rich patrons, like the Duke and Duchess Montmorency-Luxembourg, who housed, fed, clothed and defended him (the duchess hoped to one day 'merit a tiny part' of Rousseau's friendship). It also inspired the leaders of the French Revolution, who hailed Rousseau as a modern martyr for truth. The Scottish philosopher Thomas Carlyle once quipped that the second edition of Rousseau's *The Social Contract* was bound in the hides of those who mocked the first. In fact, the bourgeois revolutionaries often ignored *The Social Contract*, but Rousseau's autobiographical and fictional works—like *Confessions* and *Julie: Or, a New Heloise*—kept his portrait alive and loved. If France under the Ancien Régime was corrupt, false and selfish, this Rousseau was upright, honest and altruistic. 'Divine man', said Revolutionary leader Maximilien Robespierre, 'I have contemplated your august traits. I have understood all the sorrows of a noble life devoted to the cultivation of truth'.

But all of Rousseau's virtues, genuine and counterfeit, were prefaced by his gifts with the pen. Rousseau the author invented Rousseau the saint—and did it with boldness, lyricism and canny intelligence. When he won the Dijon Academy's prize for his essay on arts and sciences in 1750, the author's arguments—lambasting the degeneracy and weakness of intellectual life—were by no means original. Roman satirists had made the same arguments over a millennium earlier. What made the essay so striking was Rousseau's prose—what his biographer JH Huizinga described as 'the hyperbole, the defiant, not to say offensive, tone'. It gave him entry into the highest Parisian salons, his ferocity and righteousness lauded by the very aristocrats he was railing against. Rousseau had a talent, he wrote quite rightly in his *Confessions*, 'for telling useful but unwelcome truths with some vigour and courage'.

Raptures and Ecstasies

But for long spells, writing was not this best-selling author's passion. The autumn of 1765 finds Rousseau not at his study, pen in hand, but on his belly in the woods of Saint-Pierre, an island on Switzerland's Lake Bienne. Here, Rousseau was in exile.

His *Emile: or on Education* was published three years before, and greeted with condemnation and censure by Roman Catholic and Protestant authorities alike. His offence was to put heretical ideas—disbelief in original sin and revelation, amongst others—into the mouth of a Catholic vicar, and to sign the book with his own name (France was more tolerant of anonymous radicalism). His books were burned; his life was threatened, and warrants were made out for his arrest. He fled France to Motiers in Switzerland, then rushed to Saint-Pierre when his house was stoned in the middle of the night.

Ensconced in the island's woods, Rousseau looked the part of the religious iconoclast: dressed eccentrically in an Armenian robe bordered with Siberian fox, and a grey squirrel cap (more Davy Crockett than Martin Luther). To his left, on a lichen-covered rock, a copy of Carolus Linnaeus' *Systema Naturae*, the work of the great Swiss zoologist. In his right hand, a magnifying glass. Rousseau's prominent nose was only inches away from the purple flower of a self-heal, or *Prunella vulgaris*. The self-heal's pollen-covered stamens, he discovered, were long and forked—a trick of fertilisation that gave him 'joy', he said.

In this way, on the tiny island, Rousseau spent hours after breakfast, drawing and making notes, often taking home specimens to dissect or dry. He collected meticulous observations on the structure and sexual reproduction of plants, and was compiling his *Flora Peninsularis*: a study of the island's plant life. It was the most fun the infamous philosopher could have alone (*Confessions* records, in wince-worthy detail, his other solitary pursuits). 'Nothing could be more extraordinary', he reminisced in his *Reveries of the Solitary Walker*, written back in Paris, two years before his death in 1778, 'than the raptures and ecstasies I felt at every discovery'.

Guttersnipe of Genius

Saint-Pierre's plants were perfect companions for Rousseau, whose friendships were famously tempestuous.

Philosophers like Diderot respected him but eventually broke with him over his rudeness, vilification of mutual friends, and martyr fantasies. Madame d'Epinay, a patron he accused of plotting against him, later described Rousseau as a 'moral dwarf on stilts'. The Scottish philosopher David Hume, with whom Rousseau stayed in England during his exile from France, tried to secure the French author a pension from the king. For his labours, Hume was rewarded with charges of cruelty and conspiracy. 'You have brought me to England', Rousseau wrote to the baffled philosopher, 'allegedly to procure my asylum but in fact to dishonor me'. By this stage, Rousseau was showing symptoms of the madness that plagued him toward the end of his life. But even without insanity he was often tetchy and ungracious.

Rousseau also felt like an outsider in Parisian salons, and clumsy alongside the witty philosophes like Voltaire. He was too capricious and undisciplined to research and write rigorously, or cultivate his courtly demeanour. 'I abandon myself', he wrote in a letter, 'to the impression of the moment'. Unable to polish his manners or mind, but unwilling to give up his ambitions for fame, he joined the ranks of sophisticated France by attacking them, lampooning its scholars, artists and patrons, along with most of civilised France. 'Rousseau is the greatest militant lowbrow of history', wrote philosopher Isaiah Berlin, 'a kind of guttersnipe of genius'.

As a consequence, Rousseau had many educated and talented acquaintances but never felt at home in France's intellectual world. This estrangement is partly why he loved Saint-Pierre's plants. Rousseau's autobiographical works were filled with grateful descriptions of nature's silence, as against intellectual chatter. The *Prunella* did not mock his ideas, clothes or affairs; did not gossip or slander. The plants also took his mind off the threats—real and imagined—to his reputation and security. They were a simple distraction from the complications of Parisian life. 'An instinct that is natural to me averted my eyes, silenced my imagination and', he wrote in his *Reveries*, 'made me look closely for the first time at the details of the great pageant of nature'. For Rousseau, exiled from France, plants were a holiday from the strife of civilisation. Wary of more controversy, weary of endless bickering, Rousseau sought botanical diversions. The philosopher could eat breakfast, wander about Saint-Pierre until lunchtime, without spending a sou, or giving a second thought to another human being. And indeed, this was the middle-aged scholar's plan for his remaining days. 'The different soils that occurred on this island', he wrote in his *Confessions*, 'offered me a sufficient variety of plants for study and amusement for the rest of my life'.

State of Nature

But Rousseau's botanical meditations were more than curmudgeonly retreat or cheap leisure. For him, botany was a method of perceiving, recognising and recovering what he valued most: nature. It offered him respite from restlessness and the Parisian salons, but it also helped him to rediscover nature, and the best of himself.

Rousseau's basic belief was that nature was good. Not simply useful or beautiful—although it was both—but morally unimpeachable. In *Discourse on the Origins of Inequality*, Rousseau wrote that nature was the work of the 'Divine Being'. This Being, as he wrote in a famous letter to Voltaire, was benevolent, wise and perfect. Voltaire had taken issue with the metaphysical optimism of philosopher Gottfried Leibniz and poet Alexander Pope, pointing out the common and continual misery of the world. In his famous reply, published in 1756, Rousseau wrote of the 'invincible disposition of his soul', which had faith in the beneficent creator, and his works. It was partly this spiritualism that caused the break between Rousseau and the more materialist, rationalist philosophes. 'The whole', Rousseau wrote, referring to the cosmos, 'is good'. And because of this, all of nature was incapable of malice, cruelty, deceit. 'Nature ... never lies', he wrote in *Discourse on the Origins of Inequality*. Rousseau was careful to note that nature knew nothing of ethics or politics—theoretical notions of good and evil were meaningless. But he believed nature was morally exemplary nonetheless. 'All that comes from her will be true,' he said, 'nor will you meet with anything false'.

Importantly, argued Rousseau, mankind was itself honest and good, but only in the 'state of nature' before reason and the development of civilisation. For the philosopher, the first humans were naïve animals, lacking rationality and self-consciousness. But they were morally pure, without the catalogue of sins Rousseau attributed to modern France: 'wants, avidity, oppression, desires, and pride'. *Discourse on the Origins of Inequality*'s passages on the state of nature have detailed portraits of dim, muscular but noble savages who roamed the earth in a state of primitive, isolated grace. A hundred years before Rousseau's essay appeared in 1754, Thomas Hobbes' treatise *Leviathan* also sketched out a 'state of nature', but his portrait was radically different: a 'war of all against all', in which he famously saw life as 'nasty, brutish and short'. Rousseau launched a salvo of righteousness on Hobbes, arguing that the English philosopher was projecting the traits of modern man onto primal man. Before reason, Rousseau argued, mankind only followed two primordial principles: self-love and compassion. The first, *amour de soi*, kept humans alive, and allowed them to procreate: seeking food, shelter and a mate. The second, *pitié*, was what Rousseau described as 'a natural repugnance at seeing any other sensible being, and particularly any of our own species, suffer pain or death'. These two principles, the work of Rousseau's Divine Being, kept humans solitary, but also cooperative and caring when necessary. 'Compassion is a natural feeling, which, by moderating the violence of love of self in each individual', he wrote, 'contributes to the preservation of the whole species'.

The end of this idyll was marked, Rousseau argued, by social intimacy and thought. Before society, there were 'no moral relations or determinate obligations', he wrote. Pity kept men from cruelty, but they were basically amoral: aloof, thoughtless, instinctual. But the native freedom of the noble savage was lost to the needs of the community, in which natural inequalities (brains, brawn, beauty) promoted political inequalities (class, status). This bred deceit, since, if one did not have gifts, one had to pretend to have them. 'To be and to seem became two totally different things', Rousseau lamented.

Rousseau's tale of the fall of the noble savage was at the heart of his philosophy. This is why the author stressed the honesty of nature, and of man in the state of nature— the era before intelligence and community was one of brute, isolated sincerity. With thought and intimacy— that is, with society—came all the vices of modern France. Laws were introduced to overcome violence and misery, but they reinforced the rights and privileges of birth, education, beauty, wit. The poor scratched about for the basics of life, while the rich jockeyed for fame or royal favour. No-one, argued Rousseau, was happy, and all were slaves in their way:

> The [noble savage] breathes only peace and liberty; he desires only to live and be free from labour ... Civilized man, on the other hand, is always moving, sweating, toiling, and racking his brains to find still more laborious occupations: he goes on in drudgery to his last moment, and even seeks death to put himself in a position to live, or renounces life to acquire immortality.

The basic problem, for Rousseau, was that contemporary men were *against nature*. And in this, they were against themselves. They gave up their basic freedom in the state of nature to join corrupting society, and then gave it up again with unjust modern law.

Rousseau gave political and educational remedies for this malaise, each guided by his ideal of nature. In *The Social Contract*, for example, he speculated about the general will: the combined resolve of all citizens, with which they made the original social contract. As a united will, the citizens were sovereign, commanding magistrates to make laws that they themselves then obeyed; in this, the citizens were at once rulers and subjects. They lost their primitive freedom, but gained the security and power of political liberty. Born of the 'very nature of man', this general will was always right and good, and those who refused it were rightly punished.

If *The Social Contract*'s spirit buoyed readers with its bold republicanism, it was also vague, overly abstract and as totalitarian as it was liberal—citizens 'forced to be free', for example. 'They don't know what their true self is', wrote philosopher Isaiah Berlin, critically summing up Rousseau's arrogance, 'Whereas I, who am wise, who am rational, who am the great benevolent legislator, I know this'. Rousseau, who considered himself above ordinary citizens, was too enamoured with his law-giving nature to let a citizen freely depart from its commandments.

The educational recommendations of *Emile*—like breastfeeding and physical learning—were fashionable amongst aristocrats (and are regularly affirmed today, albeit with more scientific support). But the overall mood of rustic simplicity was more influential than Rousseau's child-raising advice (the Prince of Württemberg's toddler daughter developed chilblains from walking in the snow without shoes, as Rousseau had recommended). Again, as a prophet of nature, Rousseau was more important as a figurehead or literary champion than as a practical theorist, often because his diagnoses were simplistic and his prescriptions short-sighted. But in his own life, Rousseau eventually found botany as one important outlet for his ideas.

Pure Curiosity

In his essay on inequality, after all his firebrand denunciations, Rousseau suggested playfully that his critics might abandon cities for the wilderness, but he himself was stuck with modern alienation. 'Men like me', he wrote, 'whose passions have destroyed their original simplicity, who can no longer subsist on plants and acorns', simply have to live virtuously, following the two principles of nature: *amour de soi* and *pitié*. They might try to influence 'wise and good princes', and Rousseau did write a constitution for Corsica. But his most common recommendation was a kind of existential retirement: away from others, toward oneself. 'The savage lives within himself', he wrote, 'while the social man lives constantly outside himself'. In other words, Rousseau's prescription was often a meditative solitude. Good men had to stay away from fame, reputation, glory and the longing for recognition. Instead, they had to stay true to their primal nature, which promised the simple, divinely given principles of goodness. 'Virtue! Sublime science of simple minds', he asked, in *Discourse on the Moral Effects of the Arts and Sciences*. 'Are not your principles graven on every heart?'

For Rousseau, botany was one small way to rediscover these principles, by using his mind and powers of observation. In a series of letters to his friend Madame Étienne Delessert, Rousseau fleshed out these ideas. He called botany 'a pure curiosity', and stressed its uselessness. With quiet irony, he told Madame Delessert that it was not a particularly important occupation. 'It has no real utility', he wrote, 'except that a thinking, sensitive human being can draw from observing nature and the marvels of the universe'.

To rediscover nature in this way, greater observation and analysis were important—and botany was training in both. The botanist had to look carefully. The point was not to recall Latin names, argued Rousseau, but to observe keenly. 'Before teaching them to give a name to what they see', he wrote to Delessert, 'let us start by teaching them to see'. Most people, he said, never saw with sufficient clarity and discrimination, chiefly because they were wrapped up in ordinary human concerns: status, money, romance and the like. Looking at a meadow or woodland, the average Parisian simply felt some 'stupid and monotonous admiration', as the author put it in his *Confessions*. By contrast, the student of horticulture had to distinguish every anatomical detail; had to really give nature his attention. In his correspondence, Rousseau devoted a whole letter to flowers. The common daisy, for example, has a disk of tiny yellow petals, each with pistil and stamens, the female and male organs. Its white 'petals' are also flowers, each with a single forked pistil. What looks like a single ordinary flower is actually hundreds of tiny flowers, or florets. Rousseau then repeated this for dandelions, chicory, artichokes, thistle, pointing out the surprising details usually overlooked. His point, which echoed the counsel of *Emile*, was that patient, discriminating scrutiny is itself educational—it can completely change our perception. We might see the same plant every day, and be unaware of its intricacy. And suddenly, we notice more, and the novelty is rewarding. 'Sweet smells, bright colours and the most elegant shapes', wrote Rousseau, 'seem to vie for our attention'. Botany is a lesson in precise, pleasurable perception. And in this, it is a remedy for the numbed consciousness of civilised life.

Having studied the anatomy of the daisy or self-heal, the botanist progresses to physiology: what are the organs for? With Madame Delessert, Rousseau used the example of a pea. The flower is like the wrapping of a gift, with four different petals all coming together. Inside this package is a little white wall of stamens, with yellow tips on each stalk. And beneath the wall, a small green cylinder: the ovary. Why these layers of petals, stamens and pod? To protect the embryonic seed, answered Rousseau. Why is one stamen detached from the rest? It withers, to leave room for the seed to grow, answered Rousseau. In this way, Rousseau did not ask what the plant could do for him—what medicine or prestigious discovery it held. He asked instead: What does the sweet pea's flower do *for the pea*? What is the deeper pattern and purpose? In this, botany was a philosophical craft: a meditation on the basic physical and metaphysical principles, set down in nature by Rousseau's Divine Being. On this, it is worth quoting the author in full, from his *Reveries*:

> It costs me neither money nor care to roam non-chalantly from plant to plant and flower to flower, examining them, comparing their different characteristics, noting their similarities and differences, and finally studying the organization of plants so as to be able to follow the intimate working of these living mechanisms, to succeed occasionally in discovering their general laws and the reason and purpose of their varied structures, and to give myself up to the pleasure of grateful admiration of the hand that allows me to enjoy all this.

Note the breathless single sentence, which begins with economy and ends on cosmology. Here, Rousseau is lauding a kind of romantic union with nature, which overcomes the estrangement he saw in contemporary France, and in himself.

The eighteenth century witnessed a boom in horticultural discovery, cultivation and taxonomy. As the colonial powers grew, so did their herbariums and greenhouses. Acquisition, classification, exploitation: these were typically colonial pursuits. But for Rousseau, not coincidentally, this stress on usefulness was corrupt. It was destroying botany, by transforming it into a tool of human need. Medicine, for example, was blind to the beauty of the self-heal—as the name suggests, the *Prunella* was simply studied as a balm. By treating botany's insights as a reward for pure curiosity, Rousseau was trying to be less 'civilised'. Unlike his fellow citizens, *he* was treating the flower with a kind of naïve, selfless logic. He wrote of the 'great system of being' he was at one with—the 'joy and inexpressible raptures' of fusion with nature (that something was 'inexpressible' never stopped Rousseau having a good go at it).

For Rousseau, the rediscovery of these principles was also a rediscovery of himself. He believed he too had been corrupted by French society: 'If I had remained free, unknown and isolated, as nature meant me to be', Rousseau wrote in *Reveries of a Solitary Walker*, 'I should have done nothing but good'. This, of course, was a far cry from the naïve, instinctual survival of the noble savage. But, as Rousseau himself argued, there was no going back. Botany was a simple, cheap and peaceful meditation, in which the philosopher glimpsed his better self as he scaled Saint-Pierre's rocks.

Self-Heal

Botany was another example of Rousseau's talent for self-portraiture. For all his concern for education and moral reform, Rousseau was more interested in revealing than restraining himself. This is why *Confessions* continues to fascinate readers today: it leaves the vivid impression of a man's naked mind, complete with all its eccentricities and illusions. 'Self-exposure, even at the cost of revealing con-tradictory reasoning, self-delusion, and second thoughts', wrote his biographer Maurice Cranston, 'becomes its own justification'. This is Rousseau's central project.

In contrast to *Confessions*, *Reveries* and his letters, Rousseau's writings on botany reveal the author at his most gentle, modest and reasonable: not accusing well-meaning friends of betrayal, not railing against the rich with paper and ink they purchased for him, not singing the praises of parenthood while sending his children to anonymous, orphaned misery, but quietly observing, and thinking about, plants. Botany was briefly redemptive for Rousseau, because it allowed him to exercise his gifts for analysis, description and speculation, without asking him to defend his theories or polish his facade. This was not because he had discovered the 'noble savage' within, but because it removed Rousseau from the crowd, and gave him something beautiful, sophisticated and animated to contemplate. Botany was not a revelation of some perfect, God-given nature, but a reflection on nature, which provided a less awkward and threatening atmosphere for philosophy. This was solitude without loneliness, intellectual amusement without company—precisely the right medicine for 'a man unable to conceive of fraternity', as Huizinga puts it, 'or even of friendly rivalry'. In this, the traits Rousseau projected onto nature—naïve goodness, native isolation, psychological harmony—were actually traits he valued in himself, but which were most visible when there was no-one around to witness them. It is no coincidence that he was so taken with the self-heal—this is exactly what botany was for Rousseau: a self-administered remedy for the burdens of society, and of his own persona.

George Orwell: Down and Out with a Sharp Scythe

Outside my work the thing I care most about is gardening, especially vegetable gardening.
    George Orwell, autobiographical note, 17 April 1940

George Orwell looked the part of the stereotypical intellectual: stooped, spindly, wearing ill-fitting, rumpled clothes. His face also looked un-ironed—the creases of illness and overwork ('Wheezes like a concertina', said a doctor of Orwell as a child). While Orwell became an iconic modern novelist and essayist, his lifetime's illnesses were eye-wateringly Dickensian: chronic bronchitis, three bouts of pneumonia, dengue fever in Burma, haemorrhaging lungs from tuberculosis.

In the spring of 1946, Orwell had been diagnosed with tuberculosis for eight years. Instead of resting in a hospital, or 'taking a cure' in a sanatorium, he rented Barnhill, a house on Jura, an island in Scotland's Hebrides. His friend Richard Rees called Barnhill 'the most uncomfortable house in the British Isles'. Jura was equally dismal: cold, damp, remote and primitive. It was precisely where ailing Orwell was not supposed to live—a death sentence, given his infected lungs.

As soon as the author arrived, he continued in the same vein, what his biographer Jeffrey Meyers called 'his self-destructive impulse'. Instead of collapsing into bed, Orwell picked up a scythe and pickaxe. He took Jura's stony, bone-dry patches of dirt and thistles, and made a brand-new garden.

It was something of a mania for Orwell. The day after his lease began, his diary was devoted to Jura's landscape: bush fruits, azaleas, apples, *Rhododendrons*, *Fuchsias*, bluebells and wild iris. The next day, the sick writer was digging at the soil ('breaking in the turf') and planning the layout ('shall stick in salad vegetables ... bushes, rhubarb

& fruit trees'). When well enough to leave Barnhill, his Jura days were all like this: digging, fertilising, shooting, picking. Wheezing and aching, he planted lettuce and radishes. He knocked together a trestle for sawing logs, and a stone incinerator. He dried peat for fuel and killed a snake. And when he was too ill to step outdoors, the garden was still on his mind: 'Snow drops all over the place. A few tulips showing. Some wallflowers still trying to flower'. He wrote those lines in December 1949, prone in his bed, his lung bleeding. They were the last in his domestic diary. He had finished typing up his drafts of *Nineteen Eighty-Four*, and was nearly dead from the labour. He left Jura for England that very day, and never saw his island garden again. George Orwell died in a London hospital bed just over a year later, aged forty-six.

Some Kind of Saint

Orwell had talent, a good education and ambition—but at crucial moments, he invested them in what was described by his biographers as self-destructive or dead-end pursuits. Instead of studying at Oxford, he scarpered off to Burma and joined the Indian Imperial Police. He tramped and washed dishes rather than developing a secure career. Never a soldier, he left his new wife Eileen and went to fight in the Spanish Civil War. Shot in the throat by a Fascist sniper in 1937, he convalesced back at Wallington, in Hertfordshire—not with continual bed rest, but with writing and gardening ('We are going to get some more hens'). Less than a year later he was haemorrhaging and hospitalised. And on Jura, instead of resting his pale, broken body, the middle-aged author hacked at dry soil, 8 inches deep.

Meyer described this as Orwell's 'inner need to sabotage his chance for a happy life'. Troubled by chronic guilt, the author was unable to enjoy normal, middle-class contentment. He felt guilty about his privilege, his country's inequality and imperialism, and his own absence during World War I. Of course, he wasn't responsible for his father's Indian Civil Service career, or his great-grandfather's Jamaican slave-plantation profits. He did not decide on his own date of birth, too late to fight in the war. Perhaps his conscience was abnormally amplified at St Cyprian's, where the scholarship boy was taunted by rich snobs—whom he called in 'Such, Such Were the Joys' the 'armies of unalterable law'. If they lived decadently, Orwell would live austerely; if they were handsome, he would be ugly; and if they were insensitive and brutish, he would be conscientious. In short, he defined himself against their healthy, beautiful, moneyed world, and that of Eton, where he studied on a scholarship. This was the Orwell who parodied his own worst character traits in Gordon Comstock, the failed poet in *Keep the Aspidistra Flying*. Comstock showed promise, but warped pride kept him poor, parasitic on charity and deeply resentful of anyone who chased happiness. 'Failure', wrote Orwell in *The Road to Wigan Pier*, 'seemed to me to be the only virtue'. He saw virtue not only in poverty, but also in dirty, banal, draining labour—like that of the hotel staff he worked with and immortalised in *Down and Out in Paris and London*. 'At a quarter to six one woke with a sudden start', he wrote of life as a kitchen hand, 'tumbled into grease-stiffened clothes, and hurried out with dirty face and protesting muscles'. By midnight Orwell and his bed lice were back in the sack. Not the usual Etonian lifestyle.

In this light, Orwell nearly destroyed himself scything brambles and shovelling dead dirt in Jura, because he believed pain and weakness were better than idle comfort and the complicity this represented. The good life, for Orwell, was indistinguishable from gruelling, boring work. The *Aspidistra* of his novel was a symbol of this: the hardy house plant of lower-middle-class workers, which survives on little light and water. For the protagonist, Gordon Comstock, it signified laziness, conformity, conservatism: everything Orwell literally killed himself to avoid. Orwell was an atheist, but there was a religious fervour to this asceticism. Author VS Pritchett eulogised Orwell as 'some kind of saint'.

Orwell also had the monk's contempt for money, and saw gardening as a shot across the bow of expensive taste. He celebrated springtime in England as a free mass entertainment, for example. 'The pleasures of spring', he wrote in 'Some Thoughts on the Common Toad', 'are available to everybody, and cost nothing'. And birds did not pay rent, either. Likewise, in one essay he noted that the Woolworth's roses he planted in an old house decades before were flourishing—all this for six pence, he said with relish. This is a common tic of Orwell: noting the cheapness of good things, as an 'up yours' to the moneyed. Orwell 'could not blow his nose without moralising on conditions in the handkerchief industry', as Cyril Connolly once quipped. For Orwell, questions of beauty quickly turned to those of ethics, politics, economics. So, gardening was the perfect pursuit for a cultivated pauper.

Tripe and Vinegar

But there was more to his Jura gardening than a monastic complex. It was also a touchstone of truthfulness, what he called in 'Why I Write' his 'power of facing unpleasant facts'. Whatever forced Orwell to hike the path of most resistance also increased his intimacy with real life. He was a gifted author, but what raised his novels and journalism above common reportage was first-hand experience. He knew the tramps' aching bones, hunger and fatigue; the indignity and boredom of continually footslogging from workhouse to hostel. The Eton graduate had lived in a Parisian slum; had eaten disgusting tripe and vinegar in Wigan, Manchester. From his diary, 21 February 1936, living with a working-class family in northern England:

> The squalor of this house is beginning to get on my nerves. Nothing is ever cleaned or dusted, the rooms not done out till 5 in the afternoon, and the cloth never even removed from the kitchen table. At supper you still see the crumbs from breakfast. The most revolting feature is Mrs F. being always in bed on the kitchen sofa. She has a terrible habit of tearing off strips of newspaper, wiping her mouth with them and then throwing them onto the floor. Unemptied chamber-pot under the table at breakfast this morning.

Despite his crumpled dress, Orwell was a fastidiously clean man, with an unusual sensitivity to smells. But he put up with stink, filth and blowfly corpses. He was starved, soaked, flea-bitten and shot. And though guilt compelled him, he was also driven by a lust for truth. He believed it was his duty to bear witness. 'I write', he said, 'because there is some lie that I want to expose, some fact to which I want to draw attention'. What made this more than ordinary reportage was his willingness to live through the events he reported. And he did so without academic obscurantism or narrowing party loyalty. Hence his opposition to Soviet Russia against many of his fellow leftist peers, and despite his criticisms of Western capitalism. Orwell railed against English socialists' blind acceptance of Soviet and Communist policies—partly on principle as a defence of liberty, but also because he had seen first-hand the brutality of Communist forces in Spain, as they attacked Trotskyist communists and anarchists. 'I have seen the bodies of numbers of murdered men', he wrote in 'Inside the Whale': 'I don't mean killed in battle, I mean murdered'. Instead of taking communism on faith, he bore witness and reported accordingly. What mattered were facts, and Orwell intended to find them.

This is not to say that Orwell was beyond bias. He had his prejudices: Scotsmen ('whisky-swilling bastards'), homosexuals ('I am not one of your fashionable pansies') and the Catholic Church ('my obsession about R.C.s'). He could be petty, short-sighted and nasty in his prose. In *Down and Out in Paris and London*, for example, he produced caricatures of canny, greedy Jews. 'It would have been a pleasure', he wrote of one second-hand-clothing seller, 'to flatten the Jew's nose'. But bigots rarely grow out of their bigotry; to his credit, Orwell let experience change his mind. Over a decade later, with Hitler in power and millions of European Jews being slaughtered or driven to death in work camps, Orwell offered an authoritative, passionate critique of anti-Semitism. In the intervening years, the author had met many more Jews, and revised his earlier mistakes.

In this way, Orwell was the first to recognise errors of logic and fact, including his own blind spots. As a journalist, critic and novelist, his outlook was unusually contingent upon evidence, and he continually returned to particulars, details. This was a Herculean achievement, given his turbulent political era. Orwell fought passionately for his worldview—on paper and in Spain—without transforming it into the dogma of his communist and nationalist peers. In this, the author was more scientist than prophet, with a scientist's respect for facts, sceptically handled. Orwell, it could be said, *lived* experimentally.

With this scientific mindset came a respect for transparency of language. Having seen first-hand the brutality of Spain and the squalor of Paris and northern England, Orwell had no time for fancy words or high theory that obscured the facts. Hence his now famous defence of clear writing in works like 'Politics and the English Language', and the appendix on Newspeak in *1984*. Orwell argued that poor language was tied up with poor thinking. Muddled thoughts led to muddled phrases, which may seem pretty, but do nothing to illuminate the writer or reader—leading to more dubious ideas. Language, he wrote in his own typically concise prose, 'becomes ugly and inaccurate because our thoughts are foolish, but the slovenliness of our language makes it easier for us to have foolish thoughts'. For Orwell, the ability to write and think clearly was a moral responsibility. Without this clarity, words may string together nicely, but they are false.

In the appendix to *1984*, Orwell went further, describing the deliberate perversion of thought for political gain, by eradicating the richness of language. 'The purpose of Newspeak was not only to provide a medium of expression for the world-view,' he said in frighteningly cool phrases, 'but to make all other modes of thought impossible'. Orwell's insight was taken directly from the twentieth century's oligarchs and tyrants, who 'don't advertise their callousness, and ... don't speak of it as murder', he said in 'Inside the Whale': 'it is "liquidation", "elimination", or some other soothing phrase'. And it was not only the Nazis and Stalinists who did this; their English apologists also distorted the truth with sterile jargon. In 'Politics and the English Language', he referred to a university professor who was defending Soviet totalitarianism. 'A mass of Latin words falls upon the facts like soft snow,' Orwell wrote, 'blurring the outlines and covering up all the details. The great enemy of clear language is insincerity'. Orwell did not live to hear torture described as 'enhanced interrogation technique' or state-sanctioned rape as 'mandatory trans-vaginal ultrasound', but he would have recognised the bullshit immediately.

Mr Orwell: Author, Gardener, Scientist

The gardens of Wallington and Jura were at the heart of Orwell's scientific attitude and rewarded his dogged search for truth. This is because horticulture is first and foremost a realist's enterprise: it requires practical candour. A mistake with harsh frosts, for example, cannot be hidden with Politburo spin; the crops simply die. Likewise for soil, sunlight, humidity, acidity: they have tangible consequences. The labour is also unavoidably tactile: freezing mud, sharp brambles, nibbling ticks. When Orwell wanted to cultivate Jura's 'virgin jungle', as he put it, he had to suffer cold, cuts and itches. He did not want to escape from reality; he wanted to dwell in facts, however painful.

This sounds dull, but it came with genuine delight. Witness Orwell's pleasure at cheap Woolworth's roses: 'A polyantha rose labelled yellow turned out to be a deep red. Another, bought for an Albertine, was like an Albertine, but more double, and gave astonishing masses of blossom'. His diaries too were full of these discoveries. Orwell put frog spawn in a jar, just out of curiosity (they died, perhaps for want of fresh water). He made a mustard spoon from bone, and a salt spoon from a deer antler ('Bone is better'). He compared sickles and scythes for cutting rushes, and tested the right cutting angle. For Orwell, gardening was more than self-flagellation. Like all his adventures, it was an experiment—a chance to get more intimate with the facts.

As an experiment, the author's gardening was an exercise in what's called epistemology. That is, it concerned *how* we know what we know, which was fundamental for Orwell. Jura's strawberries or Wallington's lettuces did not necessarily contain some particular, predetermined truth for the author—some definite vision of man or universe. Instead, the garden was a laboratory, in which Orwell's relation to truth itself was tested. It yielded knowledge about Albertine roses or sweet Williams ('sometimes "shoot up" … but cannot be made to do so'), but it also yielded knowledge about knowledge— an outlook on reason and evidence, which recognised their strengths and weaknesses. Orwell referred to this as the 'scientific method', but he did not yearn for some utopian technocracy, populated and run by physicists and chemists. Quite the contrary. He wanted to cultivate, as he put it in *The Tribune*, 'a rational, skeptical, experimental habit of mind', for which muddy gumboots were as fundamental as a typewriter. Orwell was something of a masochist—playing scientist with a hacksaw instead of convalescing in bed. But he was also rightly passionate about the search for truth, what he called 'a method of thought which obtains verifiable results by reasoning logically from observed fact'. Faced with damaging political and military conflicts between uncritical dogmatists of every stripe—communists and capitalists, anti-Semites and Zionists, nationalists and imperialists—Orwell believed that the only hope lay in decent reason: a more careful, critical approach to truth. And he discovered this method, at least in part, in his home-built sledgehammer and a well-sharpened scythe.

For all his Etonian sangfroid, Orwell was a haunted, passionate man, who overcame frailty with impressive mental and physical labours. He had grit. And his distinctive approach is still relevant today: a familiarity with palpable reality, sceptically treated. Much of contemporary life has an atmosphere of taken-for-granted certainty to it—the conceit of flawless knowledge in key performance indicators, economic cycles, political polling, intelligence tests. What philosopher Alfred North Whitehead called 'the fallacy of misplaced concreteness'—abstractions dressed up as robust facts—is common. And this facade of perfection is regularly chased in public and private life: political slogans, psychological profiles, religious texts. It comforts us, by making life seem less uncertain and unsettling. For those with a sufficiently sceptical attitude, the garden can be a remedy for this delusion—a reminder of how subtle, changeable and complicated reality is. As Orwell discovered, 'seed plus soil plus rain plus sunshine' can be a surprisingly complicated equation, when calculated in the field. The garden is where hypotheses are only cautiously upheld—until tomorrow, when they are falsified as some unexpected variable wilts the lettuce, shrinks the gooseberries. An Orwellian garden instructs its devotees not to cling to familiar but false ideas; to be wary of all-too-perfect theories. No wonder the author of *1984* prized his gruelling Jura labours: they were a brief liberation from the totalitarian mind.

Emily Dickinson: The Acres of Perhaps

*In Childhood I never sowed a Seed unless it was
perennial—and that is why my Garden lasts.*
  Emily Dickinson, letter to Professor Joseph Chickering,
July 1885

*My nosegays are for Captives—
Dim—long expectant eyes
Fingers denied the plucking,
Patient till Paradise—*

Emily Dickinson

Amherst, New England. The Green sisters and their
brother, known for their beautiful voices, were ushered
into the Dickinson mansion. The intimidating house,
poised on 2½ acres, looked down over Main Street, across
from another 11 acres owned by Edward Dickinson.
A wealthy lawyer with ties to local civic and business
authorities, Dickinson was a man of status and standing.

But on that spring evening in 1877, he was nowhere to be seen. The siblings stood alone in the drawing room.

The Greens were invited to give a private performance, but there was no visible audience. They sang anyway: a solemn rendition of Psalm 23 ('He maketh me to lie down in green pastures …'). There was silence—and then faint applause. 'A light clapping of hands', wrote Clara Green years later, 'floated down the staircase'. The singers must have made a strong impression, for they were treated to a rare audience with Emily Dickinson, Edward's elder daughter. She had left her upstairs bedroom to speak with them in the library, dressed in her usual spectral white. Dickinson spoke breathlessly, praising their singing and reminiscing: she remembered them as children, their voices and their brother's whistle. Clara noticed 'a pair of great, dark eyes set in a small, pale, delicately chiselled face, and a little body, quaint, simple as a child'. Miss Green never saw the poet again.

Clara Green lived to a good age, and Dickinson for another ten years. But Emily rarely met visitors—in fact, she rarely met anyone. For half of her adult life, she kept to the Homestead. 'I do not cross my Father's ground', she wrote in her late thirties, 'to any House or town'. More specifically, Dickinson spent most of her free hours at a small table at her window, overlooking Main Street. She was writing: thousands of letters, notes and poems. Most authors crave a degree of solitude in order to write, but Emily Dickinson was the queen of home-bodies. Forsaking marriage, children and even ordinary family intimacy, she devoted herself to her solitary writing and reflection. Famously, she missed her own father's funeral and memorial. While mourners sat downstairs, Emily stayed in her room with the door ajar.

Of course Dickinson could not spend every daylight moment in domestic exile. She descended for household jobs, such as cleaning, canning fruits and cooking. The poet was known for her kitchen wizardry. Edward Dickinson had a penchant for her bread, and his yearly Commemoration dinner featured her famous 'black cake'. Neighbourhood children got freshly baked gingerbread, lowered in baskets from her bedroom window. Occasionally Emily was coaxed down by friends. Her correspondent Samuel Bowles once shamed her into meeting him face to face. 'Emily, you wretch!' he reportedly yelled after a long, taxing trip, 'Come down at once'. Though she could be charming or animated in company, leaving her retreat was a trial for Dickinson. She preferred her 'prison', as she called it, to close contact:

> There is a solitude of space
> A solitude of sea
> A solitude of Death, but these
> Society shall be
> Compared with that profounder site
> That polar privacy
> A soul admitted to itself—

Nosegays

Only one thing regularly, reliably seduced the recluse from upstairs: the Homestead garden. 'I was reared', she was reported as saying, 'in the garden'. This was a family pastime, particularly on her maternal side. Her mother, also Emily, was keen on Grenville roses, for example, which she transplanted from the Homestead to their North Pleasant Street address—a feat of some

horticultural dedication. As a girl, Dickinson happily
foraged in the woods for blooms ('roaming for Cardinal
flowers'), pressing, drying and labelling four to five
hundred in her herbarium book. She was also a dutiful
student of botany at high school, however much she later
doubted science's monopoly on truth ('The flower is ...
a living creature, with histories written on its leaves, and
passions breathing in its motion'). When the poet was
in her mid-twenties, she was given a new conservatory,
built beside Edward's study. Her introduction to horticulture started early, and began a lifelong attachment to
the garden.

If Dickinson had aristocratic biases, she was a dem-
ocrat horticulturally, and wasn't afraid to get her hands
dirty. Her niece, Martha Dickinson Bianchi, remembered
the adult Emily's very ordered garden: flowering shrubs,
perennials and bulbs, instead of her sister Lavinia's 'blur
of confusion'. Flowers, in particular, were sacred to the
poet. In her conservatory, she grew an eclectic menagerie
of common and foreign blossoms—from subtropical
Camellias from Asia to the ordinary carnation. 'To enjoy
such success as Dickinson's with the camellias, gardenias,
and jasmine', writes Judith Farr in her detailed study of
the poet's garden, 'requires a complex, vigilant pattern
of misting, fertilising, mulching, draining, potting, and
protecting against insects'. Visitors sometimes spied her
with her pots, kneeling on a rug—before she vanished
into the mansion as they knocked on the gate ('Presto!
she was gone', remembered one Austin Kemp, almost
sixty years afterwards).

It is hard to believe today, but in her lifetime,
Dickinson's blooms were more renowned than her stanzas.
After her death in 1886, for example, it was her flowers

that mourners chiefly recalled. To the old and sick, to grieving children and happy new mothers, Dickinson had sent thousands of her 'nosegays': small bouquets, accompanied by her poems. They consoled, cheered and celebrated those who received them. 'There are many houses … into which treasures of fruit and flowers were … sent', wrote her sister-in-law Sue Dickinson, 'that will forever miss those evidences of her unselfish consideration'. With her flowers, she was not shy; with her poems, she was forthright. Her letters to her friend Samuel Bowles were particularly flirtatious. This playfully erotic message was pinned around a pencil stub, and sent to Bowles:

> If it had no pencil,
> Would it try mine—
> Worn—now—and *dull*—sweet,
> Writing much to thee.
> If it had no word—
> Would it make the Daisy,
> Most as big as I was—
> When it plucked me?

Given the poet's era and class, Dickinson's interest in gardens was no coincidence. Gardening was a respectable and popular Victorian pastime, and provided a common language of commiseration and commemoration—books were published on the floral lexicon, and dutifully read by cultivated Americans like the Dickinsons. In this way, the poet's love of flowers and verse combined to maintain an extensive and often intense social life. If she refused to leave the Dickinson farm, she posted parts of it, and of herself, in small parcels all over New England.

Blossoms in the Brain

Emily Dickinson also had her own private symbolism, and often used the garden to express herself. An orchard was a cathedral dome, for example, while the crickets held a 'druidic' mass. The daylily spoke of immortality. 'Memory', she wrote, 'is the Sherry Flower not allowed to wilt'. She herself was a violet, a rose and the 'plucked' daisy. Beautifully, she described her poems as 'blossoms in the brain', or simply bulbs, by which she meant feats of compression. In this way, the garden was her second language.

The Homestead was also what Dickinson poeticised *about*: its beauty, the cadences and inherent drama, all contained in her father's acres. For the poet, this was a

close-knit cosmos, in which she was privy to secrets, and quiet intimacies. The tulip, for example, seeing her foot, put on its 'Carmine suit'. She saw the robins creeping and sleeping, but would not break their confidence ('Go your way and I'll go mine—'). She heard the gossip of leaves, their 'sagacious confidence'. For the housebound poet, this was more than a storehouse of literary tricks. The Dickinson Homestead was like her own private communion, and its plants and animals were the language she used to articulate this.

Not that Dickinson was traditionally religious. 'Some keep the Sabbath going to Church', Dickinson wrote, 'I keep it, staying at home'. She had no truck with conventional ideas of heaven and hell, with their threats of torture or limbo. Dickinson was horrified by the idea of eternity—as if it were an endless void, in which souls languished. In one of her most striking poems, 'Void', the poet wrote of 'neighbourhoods of pause', in which 'epoch has no basis'. Instead, Dickinson's afterlife was more Romantic, in the tradition of Emerson and Brontë. She was obsessed with what she called 'Immortality', an idea taken in part from her first mentor, the Unitarian lawyer Benjamin Newton. He taught her, she wrote, 'a faith in things unseen, and in a life again, nobler, and much more blessed'.

Dickinson, no theologian, never developed a systematic theory of this immortality. But as her private faith indicates, the garden was central to it. She often described heaven as an Eden of sorts, in which she gained literary afterlife. To her friend Henry Vaughan Emmons, for example, she wrote of her poems as flowers 'which fade not, from the garden we have not seen'. To her brother, Austin, she referred to her garden of everlasting flowers, 'where not a frost has been'. In other words, immortality was not a divine kingdom, but a kind of deathless consciousness, which survived after the grave in its 'blossoms': poems. The struggle for artistic immortality, she suggested, was like that of a northern flower fighting winter gloom and snow. 'Creator', she asked, 'shall I bloom?'

As her use of wintry metaphors suggests, Dickinson revered all the seasons, and commemorated each in verse. But her favourite season was spring, because it encouraged her belief in enduring creation. 'During March and April/ None stir abroad', she wrote, 'Without a cordial interview/ With God'. Spring bulbs, in particular, intrigued her. She was a 'Lunatic', she wrote, for this, the 'most captivating floral form'. For Dickinson, there was a mystery to the bulb's seasonal labours, but also a cosmological and existential message, which affirmed her belief in life beyond death. The daffodil, for example, died back and disappeared every winter, reappearing in spring. This mattered to Dickinson, for whom flowers were as precious as children. She grieved their loss to frost and parasites, and saw a kind of military courage and skill in staying alive. 'To be a Flower', she wrote, 'is profound/ Responsibility'. Spring, for Dickinson, was a season of bold new life for these soldiers, after periods of conservatism or annihilation. Every surviving bulb was a lesson in the possibility of a renewal.

This was a welcome message for a retiring, often lonely, sometimes ill poet, whose childhood was marked by recurrent death and sickness. Denied literary recognition by family propriety, conservative morality and her own privative character, Emily Dickinson sought immortality in her poetry and found hope for this in her

April bulbs. '"Hope" is the thing with feathers', she once wrote, 'That perches in the soul'.

'I Don't Know'

Despite her obvious fervour, the poet's belief in immortality never became doctrinaire or dogmatic. Dickinson stood out in Amherst, and eventually within her family, for her refusal to make a public profession of faith. While at the Holyoke school, she was surrounded by zealous students and teachers, pushing for her to join the congregation. This was part of a Puritan revival in New England, which hoped to save souls from the more modern Unitarianism. Over the years, her early allies—father Edward and brother Austin—were 'saved', alongside her sister Lavinia and friends. Dickinson would have none of this, which she mocked as 'flocking to the ark of safety'. Despite her longing for immortality, her doubt prevailed. Immortality was an enchanting possibility— but *only* a possibility. 'The house of Supposition,/ The Glimmering Frontier', she wrote, 'That Skirts the Acres of Perhaps—/ To me—shows insecure'. This wasn't a poetic conceit for Dickinson; she lived by it, and dealt with death accordingly. When her friend Perez Cowan's sister died, the grieving brother consoled himself with the hereafter. Dickinson replied to Cowan, an ordained minister, with brutal bluntness. 'It grieves me that you speak of Death with so much expectation', she wrote. 'Death is a wild Night and a new Road'. Time and time again she repeated this message of ignorance: there *might* be another world, and we *might* enjoy it—but there are no guarantees. 'This timid life of Evidence', she wrote, 'Keeps pleading—"I don't know"'.

This doubt was partly the tantalised eroticism that runs through Dickinson's poems. Like her celebration of solitude, Dickinson was transforming deprivation into a kind of chaste pleasure. 'Spices fly/In the receipt', she wrote, 'It was the Distance/Was savory'.

But Dickinson's distinctive doubt was also a refusal to get too carried away by abstract ideas. She was irresistibly drawn to the physical world. This was because Dickinson had, as Judith Farr puts it, 'a sensibility that found intensity delectable'. In one poem, for example, she imagined herself dead, looking back with regret for red apples, tasselled corn, pumpkins on carts. Spiritual and artistic immortality, for all its enchanting possibility, lacked this earthly immediacy. It provided her with an ideal vision of herself and what she loved—poetry, virtue, spiritual purity—but was thinner, more unreal than the living landscape of her father's farm. 'I'd like to look a little more', she wrote on another occasion, 'at such a curious earth'. In this way, the same intimacy with daffodils and bobolinks that bolstered her spiritual beliefs also kept her from committing to them fanatically.

This provides an ironic twist to Dickinson's fraught relationship with mainstream New England religion. Historically, one of the marks of Puritanism was its basic doubt: no soul, not even the most virtuous, knew if their salvation was certain. For all her monastic habits, Dickinson lived in perpetual doubt. In this, she was more Protestant than the po-faced Holyoke girls who nagged her to convert. She rejected the horror of hell and damnation, and replaced it with profound uncertainty— a gift of her father's acres, if not his library. This may be why the poet, writing to a friend, said that 'Nature is ...

perhaps a Puritan'. Elsewhere, Dickinson referred to her 'Puritan' garden.

In this, the poet's garden was a lesson in what might be called mindful transcendence: imagining her consciousness living on in language, but never fully suspending her disbelief. This involved a kind of tension—often somewhere between agony and ecstasy, in Dickinson's case—between what the mind covets and what physical reality allows. Not everyone is prone to metaphysical flights, and fewer still record them in verse. But this struggle to temper ideals is ongoing, and touches on private and public life equally: marriage, parenthood, economics and government. We need ideals, but we are easily seduced by them. The poet once referred to her literary immortality as a vast 'prize', which was imprecisely estimated 'in broken mathematics': limited, partial and biased. It's an elegant analogy, which highlights the beauty of our concepts, but also their fragile artifice. For Dickinson, the Homestead's acres were a reminder that the calculus of human imagination is always a little cracked.

Nikos Kazantzakis: Raking Stones

'What is our duty? To struggle so that a small flower
will blossom ...

Nikos Kazantzakis, *The Saviors of God*

The wiry, middle-aged man stands squinting at stones. Dressed in sensible grey slacks, sweat-stained shirt and jacket, Nikos Kazantzakis looks like an accountant on holiday in Japan. But the Greek poet, novelist and playwright, author of the brilliant *Zorba the Greek* (the eponymous hero later played by Anthony Quinn), is doing fieldwork. He has been wandering for years like this—Paris, Berlin, Italy, Spain and Russia—echoing the hero of his epic poem, *The Odyssey: A Modern Sequel*. 'Though life's an empty shade', screams Odysseus, 'I'll cram it full of earth and air, of virtue, joy, and bitterness!' Now, in the spring of 1935, Kazantzakis is still stuffing himself full with life: click-clacking clogs, sixteenth-century screens and alleys of stone lanterns. 'If only I could lift up all of Japan', he writes to his wife Eleni, back in Greece, 'and bring it to you and wrap it around your shoulders like a kimono'.

But Kazantzakis does not sail home. He stands, rooted to the spot in Kyoto's Ryoan-ji Buddhist temple, staring at a *karesansui*, or rock garden. An austere, walled rectangle measuring a modest 10 metres by 25 metres, it houses fifteen irregular rocks, placed asymmetrically in clusters on 'islands' of moss. Surrounding these is a 'sea' of pebbles, raked daily into ripples. Tapering walls give the impression of a larger space, as does the garden's use of negative space; the tiny oblong seems vast. While it borrows scenery from behind the walls—a trick known as *shakkei* in Japanese—the garden's only visible life is the moss. Everything else is dead, dry stone. Kazantzakis is captivated. 'I wander through this garden', he writes, 'and vague desires are gradually illuminated around me, crystallizing around a hard core'.

He finds beauty in the garden's austerity: its stark lines, its contrasts of moss and rock, and the undulating waves of the stones. But it also moves him because, in the *karesansui*'s stones, he sees an idealised portrait of himself. 'If I were to form my heart in the shape of a garden', he wrote in his travel book *Japan China*, 'I would make it like the rock garden'.

For all his travel exhaustion, Kazantzakis was not trying to suggest his mind was dead—that he was paralysed with exhaustion or anaesthesia. On the contrary: the rock garden left him energised. What he recognised in the *karesansui* was a metaphysical principle known as *élan vital*, or 'vital force', an idea he took chiefly from philosopher Henri Bergson, with whom he studied in Paris.

In *Creative Evolution*, Bergson compared the *élan vital* to military shells bursting into pieces, which themselves burst into pieces, and so on, forever. The fireworks show was without aim, purpose, plan: a restless, inventive principle of change. Bergson's was a so-called 'process' philosophy, part of a tradition that included the ancient Greek thinkers Heraclitus ('no man can step into the same river twice') and Cratylus, alongside modern scholars such as Friedrich Nietzsche and Alfred North Whitehead. For process philosophers, the basic metaphysical category is not being, but becoming: activity, dynamism, movement.

Kazantzakis took this basic principle and made it into a philosophical and artistic credo—what emerged from the 'form of his heart', as he contemplated the rock garden. In his literary works, he portrayed life as a continuing dialectical movement, beginning with the most primordial matter or instincts, and ending with freedom and death—and then beginning again. For example, in his book of spiritual exercises, *The Saviors of God*,

Kazantzakis described mankind's progress from childish
egotism to recognition of family, race and humanity, then
beyond humanity to all life and the cosmos as a whole.
'The universe is warm, beloved, familiar', he wrote of this
stage, 'and it smells like my own body'. This movement,
from mute impulses to meditative unity, was echoed in
Kazantzakis' modern *Odyssey*, his magnum opus, and the
book for which he hoped to be remembered. Over the
course of the poem, Odysseus moves from bestial violence
and carnality to noble militarism, to intellectual reflection, to ascetic serenity, to a sagelike welcoming of death.
Having wandered, like his author, from Europe to the
Middle East, and then to Africa, Odysseus dies willingly
in the bleak white of Antarctica. Kazantzakis describes
Odysseus' dying mind as a flame—a metaphor for pure
consciousness, without physicality. And in this flame, all
of Odysseus' memories live on for a moment more:

> As a low lantern's flame flicks in its final blaze
> then leaps above its shrivelled wick and mounts
>   aloft,
> brimming with light, and soars toward Death
>   with dazzling joy,
> so did his fierce soul leap before it vanished in air.
> The fire of memory blazed and flung long tongues
>   of flame,
> and each flame formed a face, each took a voice
>   and called
> till all life gathered in his throat and staved off
>   Death;

In this way, Odysseus climbs another rung of
Kazantzakis' metaphysical ladder, and is united with his

world. As flame, he incorporates all things into himself, and has developed beyond self and other, subject and object, and other commonsense distinctions (the entire concluding chapter of the *Odyssey* is dedicated to this philosophical climax).

But this realisation is not the end of Kazantzakis' philosophical development. Like Odysseus, his sage recognises that all is one, but then goes further: 'EVEN THIS ONE DOES NOT EXIST!'

This nihilistic concept Kazantzakis took from Zen Buddhism, and it is no coincidence that the Ryoan-ji temple was Buddhist. For Buddhists, the rock garden was not designed for sensual pleasure, but for contemplation and recognition of transient reality. Zen adepts were prompted to realise, amongst other things, the world's ephemerality, while savouring the simple poignancy of things: what the Buddhists call *tathātā*, or 'suchness'. In this, the *karesansui* was a meditative device—another of Kazantzakis' spiritual exercises: a reminder not to crave worldly things.

But while he was inspired by this vision of nothingness, Kazantzakis was not content with idle meditation or otherworldly apathy. One 'gains courage from the horror', as he put it in a letter to Emile Hourmouziós. This is why his book *The Saviors of God* concludes not with quietist monasticism, but with 'action'. The point was 'not to look passively while the spark leaps from generation to generation', he wrote, 'but to leap and to burn with it!' This 'spark' was, of course, another metaphor for his *élan vital*.

In this way, Kazantzakis' philosophy was foremost a disciplining credo, which stressed constant effort and a Buddhist refusal to covet what one's efforts achieved.

Kazantzakis was wary of comfort, pride and deference to convention, because they diminished ambition and exertion. 'The greatest sin', he wrote to his first wife, Galatéa, 'is satisfaction'. For him, *élan vital* was a grand cosmological and biological principle, but also a justification for worldly innovation: he saw himself as part of an ongoing struggle to keep shaping and reshaping reality—including the reality of himself. Hence his celebration (and sometimes deification) of perseverance and conflict. 'You're seeking God?' Kazantzakis wrote in his *Symposium*. 'Here He is! He's action, full of mistakes, gropings, perseverance and struggle. God is not the force that found eternal harmony, but the force that breaks every harmony, always seeking something higher.'

Violating their visions of godly perfection, his writings were attacked by the Orthodox and Roman Catholic churches, but Kazantzakis was not cowed. 'If you are a man of learning, fight in the skull', he wrote in *The Saviors of God*, 'kill ideas and create new ones'. This applied to his own work and life too. Kazantzakis continually strived to transform his ideas and impressions into literature, and then to overcome these in the next poem, novel or play. It was, for him, a kind of war against inertia. Witness Kazantzakis' battle cry in *Journeyings*, prefacing his travels to Europe and the Middle East: 'Words! Words! There is no other salvation! I have nothing in my power but twenty-four little lead soldiers. I will mobilize. I will raise an army'. And these soldiers, in turn, were destroyed or discarded by others, and transformed once again. 'Again the ascent begins', as he put it in *The Saviors of God*.

In this way, the *élan vital* was a metaphysical version of Kazantzakis' own daily literary and philosophical drive. 'I'd like to rest a bit', he wrote, three years before his death in 1957, 'but how? I'm in a hurry. Some voice within me is in a hurry, merciless'. Right up to the end, this was Kazantzakis' outlook: struggle, sacrifice and fleeting transformation.

A Private Sinai

Kazantzakis recognised this ideal as he contemplated the stones of Ryoan-ji: restless innovation. At first, this might look absurd: seeing primal vitality in dead stones. But for Kazantzakis, austere landscapes were precisely where the most animated, animating ideas were born. Austerity was an opportunity for *élan vital* to do its work.

This was partly because stones, in Kazantzakis' mind, were also part of the world's becoming. 'A stone is saved', he wrote in *The Saviors of God*, 'if we lift it from the mire and build it into a house, or if we chisel the spirit upon it'. Kazantzakis did not believe that stones were literally redeemed, in any Christian sense. It was a poetic way of putting his contempt for waste; for raw materials left without transformation. To develop itself, mankind had to continually labour with the world; to undertake the 'transubstantiation' of matter into new forms. 'Every man has his own circle composed of trees, animals, men, ideas', he said, 'and he is in duty bound to save this circle. If he does not save it, he cannot be saved'.

For this reason, the author believed that the most harsh places were artistically inspiring: they *forced* people to create and destroy in this way, in order to survive. Travelling in the Sinai in 1927, Kazantzakis swayed to and fro for hours on his camel, reflecting on the fate of the Hebrews, confronting 'desolate, waterless, unfriendly mountains, that despise man and repel him'. As the

Israelites endured this desert, they became tougher, more brutal. As they did, their god transformed. 'He was no longer a mass of anonymous, homeless, invisible spirits spilled into the air,' the author wrote in *Journeyings*, 'he had become Jehovah, the hard, avenging, bloodthirsty God of one race only, the God of the Hebrews'. This God, in turn, pushed the Jews to fight on, and justified their moral and political laws. As an ideal, God was the spiritualisation of the Hebrew will to survive, which arose in harsh climates. Kazantzakis also discovered this transformation in his home island of Crete, and travelling in Spain. He argued that the 'wild uninhabitable mountains' of Castile blurred reality and dream—it was a cruel, epic landscape. 'The brain seethes', he wrote in his travel book *Spain*, 'and thinks all things are easy for a willing energetic spirit'. Shaped by his own austere childhood, he believed that barrenness offered rejuvenation. The only other option was death and extinction.

Elsewhere, Kazantzakis made exactly the same point in reverse. His books are dotted with references to sweet, fertile landscapes robbing men of the urge to strive. On the Greek island of Naxos, where his family fled occupied Crete, Kazantzakis discovered a more abundant life. 'Everywhere huge piles of melons, peaches, and figs', he wrote in his autobiography *Report to Greco*, 'surrounded by a calm sea'. Naxos was comfortable and calm, but for Kazantzakis it was an unsettling invitation to complacency.

Nikos Kazantzakis was obviously a man of extremes: at once idealistic and carnal, lyrical and gritty. Half a century after his death, his intensity still comes across in his prose, rightly described by his friend Pandelis Prevelakis as 'impetuous, elliptical, and often excited'. The author's uncompromising style was captured in his stark epitaph: 'I hope for nothing. I fear nothing. I am free'. Not everyone will have Kazantzakis' obsessive work ethic, or penchant for mingling the ordinary and the metaphysical. 'Within me, even the most metaphysical problem takes on a warm physical body', he wrote in *Report to Greco*, 'which smells of sea, soil, and human sweat'.

Nonetheless, Kazantzakis' response to the Japanese *karesansui* is a striking example of a more common existential and artistic ambition. It is a reminder to keep transforming oneself and the world, while hinting at the ultimate futility of this struggle.

Three summers ago, I saw this exemplified in my late neighbour, a keen gardener. For weeks on end, he raked the stones of his gorgeous Edwardian garden. I remember him clearly: weakened by a stroke, and often unbalanced—he needed his walking frame to stay upright. But he dragged his rake over the path, pebble by pebble. It seemed pointless: day-to-day necessities—my children running to the front door, the dog galumphing back and forth, cars reversing out the gate—soon left it a mess. Surely his energies would have been better put into recuperation and recovery; into the retreat of convalescence. But he kept at it, waging his quiet war against the wayward quartz. That week, the following week, and so on— until he could no longer stand unassisted, let alone pick up the rake.

To me, this is a poignant example of Kazantzakis' philosophy. My neighbour's stones would never have budded or flowered, but they goaded him to keep transforming his path, without any promise of completion; to suffer the discomforts of age and illness, while *keeping on*. This is *élan vital*: a longing to create and destroy; to make and remake, invent and discard, even when it is seemingly useless. The dead pebbles are an invitation: to be more fully alive, while we still can.

Jean-Paul Sartre: Chestnuts and Nothingness

He ... swept aside all my suggestions that we might go for a walk. He was allergic to chlorophyll, he said, and all this lush green pasturage exhausted him. The only way he could put up with it was to forget it.

Simone de Beauvoir, *The Prime of Life*

Jean-Paul Sartre was a loser. Or so he thought. Aged twenty-nine, he was no longer a young man of promise; no longer his grandfather's golden boy. Sartre had scored the highest marks in his Sorbonne examinations, and excelled at the prestigious Paris university. Yet in 1934, he found himself teaching philosophy in Le Havre, a conservative port city in Normandy. He did not hate the town—it had its picturesque parts. But for Sartre, it was a symbol of his failure.

Sartre did his best to liven up the classroom, speaking excitedly without notes while puffing on his pipe. He played ping-pong with the boys, and stripped to the waist to box with them. The little cock-eyed philosopher was, wrote one student, 'vigorous, stimulating, amusing and serious'. But Sartre was also deeply worried: almost thirty, he felt he had achieved nothing of note. No novel, no magnum opus, not even a short story in a magazine. Over a wine at a seaside cafe with his friend and lover Simone de Beauvoir, Sartre reflected on the tedium of his life— what he called, in his war diaries, a 'doughy, abortive existence'. His career had plateaued. His friends were the same. Nothing new was on his horizon, and the same was true of de Beauvoir. 'We were both still on the right side of thirty', she wrote in *The Prime of Life*, 'and yet nothing new would ever happen to us!' For Sartre, Le Havre was a death sentence for greatness: execution by monotony.

What Filth! What Filth!

Sartre didn't yet realise that Le Havre would provide him with his two most famous characters, from the book that launched his career in 1937: *Nausea*. The first was Antoine Roquentin, *Nausea*'s misanthropic protagonist, struggling with ennui, lost love and existential anxiety. The second was a chestnut tree, in the municipal park of Bouville—a dreary port town, chiefly modelled upon Le Havre. In October 1931, Sartre sat on a bench in a public park in Le Havre and for twenty minutes contemplated this tree. He played with descriptions in his mind. When he was satisfied, he left, preparing to 'turn this tree into something different from what it is', he wrote to de Beauvoir, paraphrasing Virginia Woolf. If Sartre had de Beauvoir's romantic temperament, the tree might have become cause for reverie. In the Paris suburb of Saint-Cloud, for example, de Beauvoir was 'elated', she later wrote, by river and woodland. But not Sartre. 'Look

at the Beaver', he teased, 'in one of her trances again!'
Regardless of how 'beautiful' it was, in *Nausea* Sartre
described the chestnut tree with acute revulsion.

As Sartre told the story, Roquentin's visit to the park
was a philosophical epiphany. Not pleasant, but illuminating. For weeks Roquentin had been troubled by what
he called 'nausea', a visceral disgust and vertigo, triggered
by ordinary things: cups, food, hands. He was alienated
from others, and resentful of their easy normality. But in
Bouville's park, he finally understood the (literal and fig-
urative) roots of his problem: existence is sickening. Not
this or that existence, but being itself, the fundamental
existence of all things. And, for Roquentin (read: Sartre),
this was symbolised most powerfully by the chestnut tree.
The passage from *Nausea* is worth reading at length:

> My eyes never met anything but repletion. There
> were swarms of existences at the ends of the
> branches, existences which constantly renewed
> themselves and were never born ... I slumped on
> the bench, dazed, stunned by that profusion of
> beings without origin: bloomings, blossomings eve-
> rywhere, my ears were buzzing with existence, my
> very flesh was throbbing and opening, abandoning
> itself to the universal burgeoning, it was repulsive.

For Sartre, the tree is nauseating because it has no
reason for being. It just is. And this 'is' has a kind of stupidity to it. Not only does it just exist, without plan or purpose; it also keeps existing: growing, flowering, fruiting,
reproducing, and then it starts again. It is not that it wants
to live; the chestnut tree *cannot help living*. 'Every existent
is born without reason', says Roquentin, 'prolongs itself

out of weakness, and dies by chance'. Everywhere he looks in the park, there is this absurd being: life, which multiplies without justification. And all the meanings that are draped over beings—beauty, virtue, intimate nostalgia—are just superficial masks. Under the masks: horrifying existence, without divisions or differentiations, and which is nothing but obscene superfluity—a kind of oozing, lumpy, onto-logical playdough. The park, for Roquentin, is a house of horrors. 'What filth! What filth!' he cries.

Nausea and Nothingness

Obviously the novel was not a straightforward copy of life in Le Havre, and Roquentin was not simply a fictionalised Sartre. But at heart they were the same man. In his war diaries, Sartre wrote that Roquentin was him, with his 'living principle' removed—the author, only without his pride, passion and ambition. Roquentin's melancholy, bit-terness and revulsion—these were all Sartre's. The author had been depressed in Le Havre and had experimented with drugs: uppers to write, downers to sleep, and halluci-nogens for the adventure of it. Mescalin turned umbrellas into vultures, shoes into skeletons and, out of the corner of his eye, more squirming, oozing life: 'crabs and polyps and grimacing Things', recalled de Beauvoir in *The Prime of Life*. This darkened his mood and exhausted him.

Sartre's own nausea continued for years: in his antip-athy toward 'natural' food and landscapes, and in his writing. Six years later, when he began his existentialist opus, Sartre made nausea one of the cornerstones of his ideas. In *Being and Nothingness*, Sartre called nausea the 'taste' of the body. This needs explaining, because the book is notoriously unclear (partly fashionable German jargon, partly the amphetamines Sartre was popping). By 'body', he did not literally mean skin and bone. Rather, he meant the conscious experience of embodiment. We construct this body; it is a part of consciousness. This goes for the rest of the world too: we never touch, smell or see raw existence, what Sartre called 'being'. Sartre did not mean that there was no reality, only that *our* reality is pure consciousness. 'I want to grasp ... being,' he wrote, 'and I no longer find anything but myself'. Being has no quantities, no qualities—all these are given by consciousness. Being just *is*—this is all that can be said about it. It is contingent: unnecessary, arbitrary, meaningless. We exist by saying 'no' to this contingency. This was one of Sartre's contributions to twentieth-century thought: consciousness *is* a 'no' to pure being. It is also a 'no' to itself: it refuses its own pure being; it is divided. We split off parts of our consciousness into 'here' and 'there', 'now' and 'then'—each of these splits is a little 'nothing' within the psyche (hence the book's title).

In this way, Sartre's vision of consciousness is a kind of restless creation and destruction, which constantly invents itself and its world, then says 'no' to both, to invent them anew. For Sartre, this is freedom: we transcend our physicality and continually create ourselves, in and as consciousness. Yet Sartre still believed that we are physical beings, amongst other physical beings. This is where the body comes in. It is consciousness of this physicality, of belonging to being: the inescapable feeling of *this* time and place, with *this* height, weight and ethnicity. What Sartre described as nausea was the reminder of this meaningless contingency; the flavour of lost freedom. Everything that makes us nauseous—blood, guts, rotten meat—recalls the bodies we are trapped in.

This is why Roquentin saw the chestnut tree as disgusting. Because, while gazing at it, he had stumbled upon a philosophical axiom: anything less than pure freedom is dull, dead being, without reason or justification. And we are always thrown amongst it.

In *Nausea*, Sartre saw contingency in cups and chairs. But it was the chestnut tree that captured his imagination. This was no coincidence. For the philosopher, 'nature' was particularly worthy of indifference and disdain. He never enjoyed hiking with the Beaver and friends. While they roamed, he sat and wrote, oblivious to his picturesque surroundings. He chose canned foods over fresh. He was happiest in high, urban apartments. In an interview with *Harper's Bazaar* after World War II, de Beauvoir described the visiting French philosopher:

> He hates the country. He loathes—it isn't too strong a word—the swarming life of insects and the pullulation of plants. At most he tolerates the level sea, the unbroken desert sand, or the mineral coldness of Alpine peaks; but he feels at home only in cities.

This was obviously journalism, not philosophy—if anything, de Beauvoir was taking the mickey. And the interview was part of the popular transformation of existentialism into a fashion: cafe tete-a-tetes, black turtlenecks and jazz. This was Sartre as charismatic guru, not lifelong scholar. But de Beauvoir's description was accurate: Sartre genuinely disliked what we call 'nature', and the natural landscape. And as his chestnut-tree horrors suggest, parks and gardens did not escape his

scorn. In *Nausea*, he wrote of the 'castrated, domesti-
cated plants' growing on seaside railings. Their fat,
white leaves felt like 'gristle'—everything was fat and
white in Bouville, because of the rain. He felt besieged,
which was why he feared leaving towns: the 'Vegetation'
(note the capital 'V') clambers over everything, its green
paws grabbing and gripping. This was classic Sartre, like
something from an old *Doctor Who* episode: assailed by
lurking lamb's ear.

So for the philosopher, plants were a symbol of being.
And being was contingency: pure existence, without free
consciousness. What made Sartre's vision unique was the
unhappy mood of this symbol: nausea. This was a gut
response that did not occur with thinkers he admired.
German philosopher Martin Heidegger, for example, was a

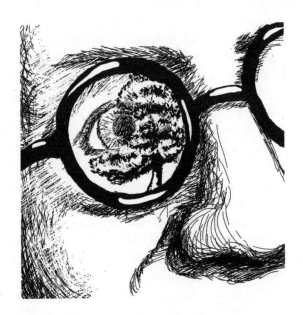

profound influence on Sartre. He said he began Heidegger's *Being and Time* in the 1930s, then studied it more keenly as a Stalag prisoner in World War II (Heidegger's prose warrants a captive audience). More than any other modern philosopher, Heidegger most strikingly and systematically portrayed humanity as a brief flare-up of meaning in an otherwise meaningless cosmos. But while Heidegger recognised the anxiety of our responsibility, he never flinched from being; that is, from the bare fact of existence. In his later works particularly, Heidegger expressed an awed astonishment—being as something worthy of reverence, not disgust. In his 1955 'Memorial Lecture', for example, he wrote that we step back from being—not as a retreat, but as if we were stopping, amazed, to admire the view. And not uncoincidentally, the German scholar was devoted to precisely the rustic landscape Sartre loathed: woodlands, streams, humble peasant cottages. Sartre specifically avoided hikes with de Beauvoir and friends, whereas Heidegger often took a break from writing to hike—he even had his own kitschy Black Forest hut. So Sartre's strange loathing was not influenced by basic philosophical principles; by his recognition, following Heidegger, of humanity's leap from being. The Frenchman's queasiness was his own, distinctive trait.

Sartre was notoriously cavalier about others' bodily ailments. During a boat trip in Greece, de Beauvoir vomited in the choppy water. Sartre 'remained quite unmoved by my spasms of retching', wrote de Beauvoir in *The Prime of Life*, 'which he ascribed to deliberate malice on my part'. For all his drug abuse and illnesses, the paunchy philosopher did indeed have a tough constitution. But philosophically, Sartre was made of weaker stuff than Heidegger, and perhaps de Beauvoir. When it came to being in general, and creeping, oozing plants in particular, Sartre was sick to his stomach.

The Little Toad

Sartre's nausea began in childhood. His earlier works stressed the radical freedom of consciousness. It was, he argued, its own rootless origin. But later on, the philosopher started a more Freudian analysis, tracing the scars left by childhood trauma. In his analyses of himself and others—Gustave Flaubert and Jean Genet—he sketched his psychological evolution. The result is not always convincing, but subsequent biographers confirm the key points.

In his autobiography, *Words,* Sartre recalls how feminine he was as a toddler. Dressed as a little girl, mollycoddled, decorated with long blond ringlets, he never learnt how to be valued for typical masculine traits. He was loved for his cuteness and his chatty playfulness. When his grandfather, the dominating Charles Schweitzer, cut off his curls, this changed: his unattractiveness was obvious, to the adults and to Sartre. Suddenly, the golden boy was gone, replaced by a squinting 'toad', with a puny body and a wandering right eye. The story of Sartre's growing disenchantment with himself ended with a visit to the Jardin du Luxembourg, in Paris. No-one played with him. To the other children, he was neither beautiful nor strong nor brave—certainly not the hero of his favourite adventure stories. He was just a small, ugly, awkward boy. This was not mockery or hatred; it was worse: he was invisible. 'I had met my true judges,' he wrote, 'and their indifference condemned me. I never got over being unmasked by them: neither a wonder nor a jelly-fish, but a shrimp that interested no-one'. All that

Sartre could not control—his body, his face, his physicality—had let him down, and he hated them. He was perceived, he wrote in his *War Diaries*, as 'an obscene goat'. Nature had failed him.

As Sartre tells the story, the grandfather who precipitated this crisis also offered the cure: culture. Charles Schweitzer was an educated man: a German teacher and author of textbooks who loved the French language. He encouraged the boy to read—classic French and German novels, the encyclopaedia, Jules Verne—and, more importantly, to write. And write he did: poems, essays, novels—for the rest of his long life, Sartre was a prolific author, churning out some twenty pages a day. While Sartre's school grades waxed and waned with his mood and domestic circumstances, the boy was clearly intellectually gifted and combined this with a sharp wit and a passion for words. His grandfather and mother dutifully applauded, only their praise was no longer for his cutesy Shirley Temple show but for his literary performance. Later, as a teenager, Sartre realised he could also impress schoolmates and girls with his words. 'Writing was a form of seduction', writes biographer Ronald Hayman, 'the aim was to peel away the mystery of things and offer them in all their splendour to a girl'. At the same time, Sartre also began to write for himself. It was still a performance, but it was one he was able to witness and judge. 'By writing, I existed', he wrote in *Words*, 'I escaped from the grown-ups; but I existed only to write and if I said: me—that meant the me who wrote'. Trying to play in the Jardin du Luxembourg, he was a failure: an outsider, an 'ugly little toad'. Trying to impress one Lisette on a floral avenue in La Rochelle, the boy was 'a bum with one eye that says shit to the other'. But in a study, a library, a schoolroom, a cafe, Sartre dominated. Culture succeeded where nature failed, and he hated the latter for it.

The point is not one of simple association: that the Luxembourg Gardens were tainted by Sartre's feelings of rejection, and therefore all gardens were. Instead, it was one episode in an ongoing struggle to be loved and valued. As he described it, this caused a profound split within Sartre between, on the one hand, all that he was proud of—his bright mind, his clownish performance, his literary gifts—and, on the other, all that embarrassed or pained him: his physique and the workings of his body. He had supreme confidence in his voice, ideas, humour— they won him many beautiful women, by whom he liked to be surrounded. But Sartre rarely enjoyed sex, precisely because of its physicality. His frankly oddball passages on slime, in *Being and Nothingness*, are simultaneously damning of sap, semen and sex—slime as 'sickly-sweet feminine revenge'. He was clearly bothered by sex, and also believed that a lover could get no pleasure from *his* body. He was uncomfortable with the reflexes of arousal and described himself as 'more a masturbator than a copulator'. Better than both, he loved to *write* about it all at length in letters posted to de Beauvoir. 'Sartre fucked Bianca', writes philosopher Bernard-Henri Lévy, about one early conquest, 'but he climaxed with the Beaver'.

In this, Sartre was an absolutist—in life, as in philosophy. As he argued in *Being and Nothingness*, his freedom was absolute: all that won him approval was infinite. It is like a schoolboy's dream of superhuman power, only the potency is cognitive, not muscular. And all that oppressed him was absolute other. He took those parts of himself that were loathsome and exiled them completely. They became pure being: stupid, unjustified, disgusting. 'This ugliness, this absolute disaster that it induces in the economy and harmony of Being', writes Lévy, 'convinced him of the invincible darkness of things and of the consequent impossibility of reconciling the world to himself'. This is why Sartre wrote nausea into the Le Havre park and cemented it in the foundations of his philosophy: the chestnut tree was part of nature, which he had withdrawn from himself and put on the other side of an ontological abyss. Heidegger worshipped being and nature; his most famous French student vilified both.

Taken as a retreat from discomfort, awkwardness and embarrassment, Sartre's philosophy looks less like the polished theory of a free mind and more like an organism protecting itself. Put simply, this is not the work of pure consciousness. Sartre's consciousness was riddled with instincts and impulses, which were as biological as they were cognitive. In fleeing from his body in particular, and nature as a whole, he demonstrated the unavoidable influence of both. In one of those ironies that make hypocrites of most philosophers, Sartre's chestnut-tree nausea was an exemplary case of bad faith.

Growing Up

Simone de Beauvoir's experience was exactly the opposite of Sartre's. In her autobiographical books, she wrote freely of her delight in the Limousin landscape, capturing a child's simple reveries ('Under the thorny hedgerows and in the heart of the woods', she wrote in *Memoirs of a Dutiful Daughter*, 'were hidden treasures'). Her love for nature deepened as she aged, and faced adult love, war, poverty and loss. After World War II, de Beauvoir wrote to Sartre from Gary, Indiana, where she was staying with her lover, American author Nelson Algren. With Algren, she had enjoyed what was impossible to savour with Sartre: hiking, and passionate afternoons in bed. Amidst the usual gossip and political lamentations, she reflected on her simple happiness 'in the garden, with a little lake at my feet'.

De Beauvoir had the courage to embrace physicality: her own and that of the world at large. This is not to say that she wasn't informed by Sartre's existentialism. In her influential feminist masterwork *The Second Sex*, de Beauvoir saw the body not as the whole of a woman's being, but as, in her words, 'a limiting factor for our projects'. The body 'is not enough to define her as a woman', she wrote, 'there is no true living reality except as manifested by the conscious individual through activities and in the bosom of society'. This was a classic Sartrean idea. What kept women from economic and professional equality was not childbirth, but very specific social and psychological conditions. Likewise, de Beauvoir catalogued the oozing, spasming, bleeding ('the bloody verdict') female body—shades of Sartre's passages on slime. But unlike her friend, she saw our bodies as inexorably intertwined with our minds. There was no realm of pure freedom— the body impinged. She recognised that her consciousness was a mongrel, not Sartre's pure breed. 'If you gave way to tears or nerves or seasickness', de Beauvoir wrote of Sartre, in *The Prime of Life*, 'he said ... you were simply being weak. I ... claimed that stomach and tear ducts, indeed the head itself, were all subject to irresistible forces on occasion'. De Beauvoir acknowledged that, like Le Havre's park, her psyche contained blind, dim, thoughtless processes and principles—Sartre's 'being'. And when de Beauvoir enjoyed, as a girl, 'weeping willows, magnolias, monkey-puzzles', she was revelling in this, the being Sartre loathed.

For all his fear and loathing, Sartre led a full life, and was loved obsessively by many. As a man, the philosopher could be funny, moving, intriguing—a conversational and intellectual dynamo. He was exploitative and deceptive with women, but also generous and loyal. Decades of denying his body eventually left Sartre dizzy, lame, blind and incontinent—but de Beauvoir, along with his other girlfriends, stoically dealt with the prescriptions and whisky bottles. For over a quarter of a century, her letters read as professions of adoration: from the 'hundred kisses' of 1930 to the 'big hug and kisses' of 1955, de Beauvoir was a faithful friend to her 'dear little being'. As he seduced beauties in France and abroad, she endured his evasions and betrayals. If he was a 'bit of a tomb', as he put it to de Beauvoir's later companion Claude Lanzmann, the stink of death did not turn his lovers' stomachs.

As a writer, Sartre was a novelist of rare power and a bold journalist. Throughout his career, he remained committed to writing, even when he had forgotten his audience. If not the most original or influential scholar, Sartre was certainly the most famous philosopher of the century—the archetypal public intellectual. Fifty thousand fans crowded his funeral, and his name spearheaded the existentialist fashion of the 1950s. There are many names that are only remembered because of his. Sartre's lopsided philosophy did not rob him of rightful success or fame. His flaws, in philosophy and life, were consistent in this respect. The point is this: Jean-Paul Sartre was the quintessential modern, urban thinker, for whom gardens were somewhere between dull and disgusting. And he did not miss what he lost.

Voltaire: The Best of All Possible Estates

Life is bristling with thorns, and I know no other remedy than to cultivate one's garden.
>Voltaire, letter to Pierre-Joseph de Boisjermain,
>October 1769

Tend your vines, and crush the horror.
>Voltaire, letter to Jean d'Alembert, February 1764

Wearing a thick fur coat, five silk caps and a woollen hat, Voltaire sits in his 'cabinet': not a luxurious study or a private chamber in his neoclassical mansion but a bench under an old linden tree. Afternoon sunshine has warmed the air, but the 'monarch of French literature', as James Boswell described him, is still shivering a little. In his mid-seventies, the great Enlightenment author—essayist, playwright, poet, satirist—is skin and bone (and nose, as the caricaturists remind him). As he sits and writes, he continually shifts on his seat—the prostate cancer that will kill him in seven years, in 1778, has already begun. But he keeps writing. Hidden by pergolas, seated just beyond the gravel and grass walks of his Ferney estate, he looks like a bourgeois retiree, writing instructions for his twenty-three gardeners or negotiating another lucrative loan. But what compels the wealthy septuagenarian to leave his sixteen-bedroom chateau is not household management or commerce. In his garden cabinet, Voltaire is living up to the motto he adopted in Prussia, as the kept philosopher of Frederick the Great: *écrasez l'infâme*, 'crush the horror!'

The *infâme* was Voltaire's nickname for what, in any era, destroys liberty and retards thinking. In his time, it was an alliance of fanatical state religion and French

absolutism, which offended the author's moral principles
and caused him much public and private grief. For most
of the eighteenth century, France was officially a Roman
Catholic country. Church rituals, dogma and superstition
ruled with little judicial redress, and the law itself was
prejudiced in letter and application. Over his long life,
Voltaire grew increasingly infuriated by oppression of
innocent French citizens. For example, his friend and lover
Adrienne Lecouvreur was denied a Christian burial. Her
crime: working as an actress. While monarchs and aristocrats guiltlessly took parts in Voltaire's plays, talented
women like Lecouvreur were reviled as little more than
prostitutes by priests, the aristocracy and French citizens
alike. Aged just thirty-seven, and despite Voltaire's frantic
lobbying, Lecouvreur was dumped in a pauper's grave in a
wasteland on the Paris outskirts. Her English peer, actress
Anne Oldfield, was buried only months later, in October
1730, in Westminster Abbey. For Voltaire, this pointless
tragedy was the work of *l'infâme*. The same church and
state alliance stopped official publication of Voltaire's epic
poem in praise of former Protestant King Henry IV, the
Henriade. *L'infâme* also threatened Voltaire with impris-
onment in the Bastille, without trial or judgement by his
peers, for publishing the *Henriade* secretly. He had it
printed in the more progressive, Protestant Netherlands,
then smuggled into Paris in a wagon carrying furniture
and on pack horses. For Voltaire, eighteenth-century
France combined the worst of religious superstition—
communion, petitionary prayer, holy wars, and beliefs
like original sin—with foolish kings, malicious clergy and
a corrupt *parlement*.

To fight the horror, Voltaire—baptised François-Marie
Arouet—became a dogged reformer, philanthropist and

provocateur. His aim was simple enough: 'Less superstition, less fanaticism; and less fanaticism, less misery'.
While he did believe in God as the supreme creator, he
lambasted the Church, which he saw as a kind of grand
debauch. He poked fun at the monarchy, advocated for
persecuted Protestants and invested heavily in local busi-
nesses and infrastructure. With ardour that still invites
readers to laugh alongside him, Voltaire never missed an
opportunity for a dig at the priests. In 1764, American
doctor John Morgan visited him at Ferney and was sur-
prised at his venerable host's fury against the French
Church. 'Hate hypocrisy, the masses', he fumed, 'and
above all hate the priests'. James Boswell described Voltaire
getting so steamed up at the clergy, 'like an orator of
ancient Rome', that he almost fainted. Even his plays—
aside from those sucking up to the French court—were
jabs at religious bigotry. He believed that even the cruel-
lest zealots would weep if they saw their own crimes on
stage. 'Tears', he aphorised in his philosophical dictionary, 'are the mute language of sorrow'. But Voltaire had
more up his sleeve than melodrama. Somewhere between
columnist and stand-up comedian, he also skewered his
peers with satire and quips. 'No one has ever been so
witty as you are in trying to turn us into brutes', he gibed
at Jean-Jacques Rousseau, 'to read your book makes one
long to go on all fours'.

For all his public debates, Voltaire was not committed to academic niceties ('All the philosophers were
unintelligible', he quipped). He wanted to drive change:
in minds, and increasingly in French laws, technology and
behaviour. 'There is a point beyond which research satis-
fies only curiosity', he wrote in his *Philosophical Letters*,
finished after his return from relatively free-thinking and

tolerant England, in 1729: 'those ingenious and useless truths resemble stars that are too far from us to give us any light'. In this, Voltaire was not a philosopher in the more modern sense—a systematic theorist, disinterestedly pursuing truth for its own sake. He was closer to the ancient Greek philosophers like Socrates and the Stoics: interested in science and the nature of reality, but more concerned with using reason to improve themselves and society—what the eighteenth-century French called a philosophe. 'Man is born for action', he wrote against the Christian philosopher and mathematician Blaise Pascal, 'as sparks fly upwards ... Not to be active and not to exist are the same thing for mankind'. And Voltaire had more spark than most.

'Let Us Cultivate Our Garden'

For Voltaire, the gardens of Ferney were an emblem of his 'action'; of altruistic local reform, opposed to a stubborn conservatism. He made this statement boldly in his story *Candide,* published in 1759, just after he settled at Ferney. The butt of his book-long joke is a kind of metaphysical optimism, voiced by Dr Pangloss, who is a stand-in for philosopher Gottfried Leibniz and others, including Voltaire's younger contemporary Jean-Jacques Rousseau. Pangloss believes that this world is the best of all possible worlds, in which 'everything is best', cosmically speaking. Rape, torture, poverty, starvation might *seem* like the work of a cruel or incompetent deity, but they are just parts of a magnificent whole (we might call them 'metaphysical collateral damage'). When combined with widespread inequality and injustice, this philosophy sent a profoundly conservative message: ignore the world's brutality, because all is for the best. Voltaire showed his hero, Candide, naively accepting these platitudes, then being forced to confront their absurdity. After witnessing a series of horrors, and suffering many himself, Candide rejects 'metaphysico-theologico-cosmolo-nigological' shenanigans in favour of what looks like a retreat into a quiet life. His final retort to Pangloss is now famous: 'Let us cultivate our garden'.

At first, this looks like a limp riposte to suffering— a disengagement from the world, out of step with his well-deserved reputation as a literary duellist. And it's true that Voltaire did write much of *Candide* at Ferney, well removed from the king's court and *parlement*. Having already seen the inside of a Bastille cell, and endured exile from Paris, Voltaire was determined to evade the French authorities. Pays de Gey, where Ferney was situated, was far from the seats of power in Paris and Versailles, and close to the border if he needed to escape to Switzerland or the Prussian protectorate of Neuchâtel. Having spent much of his youth and middle age moving from one patron to another, and at the mercy of local lords and clergy, Voltaire learnt that distance could safeguard his literary freedom. King Frederick of Prussia once referred to the philosophe as an orange, to be squeezed for amusement, then thrown away. Voltaire resolved to 'place the orange peel in safe keeping'. When he purchased Les Délices ('The Delights') he was upfront about these interests. 'I speak what I think', he wrote from Les Délices, 'and do as I will'. At Ferney, just inside the French border, Voltaire was having his brioche and eating it: the security of Switzerland, but on his native soil.

Voltaire was also using his estates to avoid the distractions of fame. By the time he purchased Ferney in his sixties, Voltaire was less a celebrity and more a literary Olympian. He arrived at Ferney and Tourney in a luxury coach, dressed in crimson velvet and ermine, and was greeted with bouquets, baskets of oranges and a cannon salute. Over the year he received visitors like a king at court, particularly English and Scots travellers on their Grand Tour (one hundred and fifty Englishmen in a decade, his biographer Roger Pearson reports). 'For fourteen years now', he wrote in 1768, 'I have been the innkeeper of Europe'. Because of this popularity, and his duties as a landlord and philanthropist, Voltaire was regularly interrupted. His Ferney walks and arbours provided pleasant asylum from the many guests at his own chateau. At his bench, hidden by 'evergreen hedges', Voltaire reclaimed the solitude and silence he had lost to fame.

But for Voltaire, the garden did not symbolise monkish quietism—quite the contrary. It certainly shielded him from attacks and distractions, but it was also a bold metaphor for compassion, responsibility and pragmatism—a call to improve his immediate surroundings. Voltaire argued that the world was marred by misery and cruelty, and no benevolent, all-powerful god would ever arrive to tidy up the mess. There was no great plan—no providence—and certainly no divine mandate for kings and clergy. But this, for Voltaire, was not cause for cynicism or fatalism. Nature gave humankind reason and hope, and it was up to us to improve our lot. Instead of toying with grand philosophical systems, or becoming mad with power, we ought to start within our own sphere of influence: our marriages, children, towns and humble backyards. Hence Voltaire's commitment to his estate. The wheat of Ferney would not miraculously grow itself; to provide the bread at the baron's table, the fields had to be planted and

reaped, year after year. Ferney required practical exper-
tise, continual labour, and devotion. And likewise for
civil institutions: the estate stood for France as a whole,
which deserved to be governed wisely, benevolently, toler-
antly. This is the point of Voltaire's conclusion: Candide's
garden required careful, attentive custodianship—one
that nurtured the community as well as the soil.

This wasn't just a literary flourish in *Candide*.
Horticulture was an ongoing theme in Voltaire's correspondence, particularly when encouraging reform. Writing
to the mathematician and Encyclopedist Jean d'Alembert,
for example, Voltaire argued that the time was right to
'topple the colossus' of religions and tyranny. 'Tend your
vines', Voltaire told d'Alembert in 1764, 'and crush the
horror'. This metaphor was used regularly in Voltaire's
letters to the Encyclopedists, along with images of fruits,
flowers and 'sowing the good grain'. For Voltaire, gardening and enlightened reform were part of the same
project: the use of one's natural intelligence to promote
liberty and opportunity. To 'cultivate one's garden' was
to make *this* world, right here and now, a little better.

Importantly, Voltaire's chateau gardens were practical
examples of this, *Candide*'s message of progressive custodianship. They did not merely symbolise the Enlightenment:
they *were* it. In 1735, before he purchased Ferney, the
author set up house in Cirey, the rural mansion of his then-
lover, mathematician and scientist Émilie du Châtelet. The
couple planned the grounds together and bickered happily about it. 'She has limes planted where I had settled on
elms', grumbled Voltaire to the Comtesse de la Neuville in
1734: 'she has changed what I made into a vegetable plot
into a flower garden'. It was a form of independence, but

also of altruistic improvement—and it stuck with Voltaire, well after Émilie's tragic early death. In 1755, Voltaire and his new companion (and niece) Madame Denis moved into Les Délices in Geneva. Immediately, they saw to the gardens. They ordered flowers and herbs, grew asparagus and artichokes in the greenhouse, and planted apple, peach and pear trees. For the landlord, this was more than an amusement: it was a way to take responsibility for himself and others. He pictured himself not simply as a free author or an entitled king but as a generous elder. 'Here I am', wrote Voltaire in the spring of 1755, with a touch of anti-ecclesiastical irony, 'finally leading the life of a patriarch'. Voltaire even offered Jean-Jacques Rousseau, whose ideas he lampooned, Les Délices' amenities: freedom, soft grass and 'the milk of cows' (Rousseau, predictably, declined).

At Ferney and Tourney (a sister estate, 3 miles away), Voltaire was more industrious still. In keeping with his commitment, he drained marshes, fertilised and sowed fields, and planted vines. Much of his estate's produce ended up on the banquet table for his many guests. 'Show me in history or fable, a famous poet of seventy who has acted in his own plays, and has closed the scene with a supper and ball for a hundred people', wrote visitor Edward Gibbon in 1763. 'I think the last is the more extraordinary of the two.' (The author of *The Decline and Fall of the Roman Empire* probably knew a thing or two about feasts.) Voltaire even kept a plot close to the Ferney chateau, which he worked personally— 'M. de Voltaire's field', it was called. Formal gardens were also carefully arranged, alongside parkland planted with oak, linden and poplar—including the landlord's pergola cabinet, with silkworms nearby (perhaps the source of his many caps).

Alongside his campaigns for judicial reform and human rights, Ferney and Tourney were a vital part of Voltaire's struggle against *l'infâme*—the campaign to leave his France better than he found it. If Kings Louis XV and Frederick, busy with imperial warmongering and profiteering, would not improve their territories, Voltaire would at least see to his.

The Voice of Nature

Gardens, in this way, were symbols and examples of Voltaire's ethical project. They also inspired him to keep working at it. To do this, they presented him with a vision of nature's intricacy and grandeur. As a deist, Voltaire was convinced by the argument from design: a universe this elegant was not the result of chance. 'The world is assuredly an admirable machine', he wrote in his *Philosophical Dictionary*, 'therefore there is in the world an admirable intelligence'. So in Ferney's sunrises and its fields, Voltaire saw a deeper pattern: not a revelation of Church doctrine, or the divine right of kings, but of godly beauty and intelligence. And this recognition, in turn, held a message of goodwill and responsibility: toward a sacred but imperfect and unpredictable universe. It was not the best of all possible worlds, in which 'all was well'. But it was well designed, and amenable to tinkering. With brains, elbow grease and goodwill, it could become better. In his 1763 'Treatise on Tolerance', Voltaire summed up this philosophy, putting his own credo into the mouth of nature itself:

> I have given you strength to cultivate the earth, and a little glimmer of reason to guide you; I have implanted in your hearts an element of

compassion to enable you to assist one another in supporting life.

By meditating upon nature in this way, Voltaire was moved to continue his reforms; to keep labouring, despite the fact that he no longer had the best of all possible eyes, teeth and digestion. The earth was not telling him to pray for God's grace, or to burn heretics for their unorthodox metaphysics ('Almost everything that goes beyond worship of the Supreme Being and the heart's submission to its eternal order', he wrote, 'is superstition'). The fields and lindens of Ferney had a more progressive message: François-Marie, tend to your vines already.

So for Voltaire, security and peace were part of a more profound commitment to responsible, rational progress, and the goods of nature that enriched and encouraged this. If Ferney became the philosophe's best possible world, this was not because of a god's love or a king's favour. It was because M. Voltaire, like his Candide, had indeed cultivated his gardens—and they him.

A Stranger at the Gates

*Isn't the freshness of the air most welcome and
pleasant ... And as a crowning delight the grass, thick
enough on a gentle slope to rest your head on most
comfortably.*

Socrates, in Plato's *Phaedrus*

His fondness for hemlock notwithstanding, Socrates was
not known for his botanical interests. 'The men who dwell
in the city are my teachers,' he told his friend Phaedrus, 'not
the trees or country'. Yes, Socrates was happy alfresco—
wandering Athens in winter wearing only a light robe. But
his mission was overtly about human interests. Morality
was more important than biology or physics: 'know thy-
self' was his Delphic motto. To refine his ideas, Socrates
wanted conversation and debate with fellow free men, not
strolls in the fields. For this reason, the philosopher rarely
left the city walls. He founded no Lyceum or Academy—
his regular classroom was the *agora*, Athens' marketplace.

But Plato left a noteworthy dialogue, *Phaedrus*, in
which Socrates sang one garden's praises. Socrates' brief

flirtation with a sacred grove is a surprising testament to the garden's intellectual value.

Socrates Gets Possessed

As Plato tells the story, Socrates was coaxed into the countryside by his friend Phaedrus, who promised to read aloud a new essay by the scholar Lysias. Phaedrus was walking on doctor's orders, Socrates out of curiosity. They strolled to a sacred grove by the banks of the Ilissus River, just outside Athens' walls. As Christopher Thacker notes in his *History of Gardens*, groves were

progenitors of the classical garden. They had an aura of primordial sanctity: marked off from the city on the one hand and the wilderness on the other, and often decorated with altars and statues.

Socrates, who had shown little interest in groves or woodlands, sat by the Ilissus River and found himself overcome by a bizarre lyricism. 'Upon my word, a delightful resting place, with the tall, spreading plane,' he told a gobsmacked Phaedrus, 'and a lovely shade from the high branches of the *agnos*. Now that it's in full flower, it will make the place ever so fragrant'. Throughout the dialogue, Socrates professed to be touched by the spirits of the grove. He called on the Muses for help with his speech and spoke of a 'divine presence' animating him. At one point, he referred to his style as 'dithyrambic'—evoking the verses traditionally inspired by Dionysus, often in sacred groves.

Even with Socrates' trademark irony, the atmosphere of the dialogue is lyrical—a departure from his usual sober logic and dry wit. *Phaedrus* was also a change for Plato himself, who was wary of physicality and the bodily senses. In *Phaedo*, for example, he argued that the soul was 'led astray' by the body. The true philosopher had to overcome the flesh, insofar as this was possible. Yet by the banks of the Ilissus, he had Socrates possessed by 'divine madness', praising the physical world that the author often disdained: the breeze, cicada chorus and 'pillow' of grass. Overcome, Socrates explained that poetic possession 'seizes a tender, virgin soul and stimulates it to rapt passionate expression'. Like the beauty of a lover, spirits in the countryside can help the poet to glimpse ultimate reality: Plato's divine ideas, instead of the illusions of ordinary life. The point is not that Socrates was being a lyricist as he spoke, but that, for the old gadfly and his student, the grove offered a transcendent vision, unavailable in the marketplace or gymnasium. With its sacred mood, it inspired Socrates' reflections—and viscerally so. He did not merely think of the connections between madness, beauty and truth; he felt them, as if his body were taken over.

The exact mechanism of Socrates' epiphany is neither here nor there. Plato's explanations are often more mythic than scientific, and have a supernaturalism that sticks in the craw of many modern thinkers. But despite this, *Phaedrus* is a striking record of the garden's philosophical potential. For Socrates, the grove's beauty was aesthetic bait on the hook of reverie and reflection. Phaedrus remarked that Socrates was like a 'stranger' passing through the gates, seeing his city for the first time. The grove's boundaries, in other words, encouraged a change of mind. All the philosopher had to do was *look again*, with this characteristic receptivity and acumen.

Just Beyond ...

For Plato, Socrates' possession seemingly had practical consequences. Some thirty years later, he opened his school near the consecrated grave of the hero Akademos, also by the city walls. Just over a decade after Plato's death, his student Aristotle opened the Lyceum, not far from the Ilissus River. Since the Classical era, as we have seen, a great many philosophers, novelists and poets have followed suit, seeking something unavailable in a Sussex sitting room, Basel university hall or Paris apartment. They have made the garden their intellectual and artistic collaborator—a silent partner of sorts.

Some, like Woolf, Orwell, Dickinson, Austen and Voltaire, regularly got their fingernails dirty. Others, like Proust and the elderly Colette, compensated for feelings of alienation with their imaginations. Others still, like Kazantzakis, Rousseau and Nietzsche, were chiefly content to observe and reflect. What they had in common with Plato, and with one another, was a commitment to the life of the mind, and the recognition that this was enhanced and enriched by the garden. For over two millennia, it has consoled some with deist awe, while confronting others with godless anarchy; it has calmed, emboldened and edified.

The point is not that profound thought requires bonsai, apple orchards or raked stones; that every arborist is an Aristotle. As Sartre's rejection of nature demonstrates, the garden is not necessary for philosophy or a life of intellectual freedom. The garden simply offers an opportunity: for distinctive meditation and contemplation. And it need not be grand or exotic to do this. For all the talk of 'great estates', the garden's ordinariness is a virtue: the mystery is rarely far away. This philosophical companion still waits, as it did for Socrates, just beyond the gates.

Bibliography: Leafing

In *On Reading* (Souvenir Press, 1972), Marcel Proust describes himself as a child, looking for a reading nook in a maze of hedges. Near 'the asparagus bed, the strawberry edgings, the pond', he was able to read in silence, undetected and undisturbed by parents (or servants).

One of Proust's points, in this typically rambling but charming essay, is that books are often mementos of lost gardens—we remember, not always the exact words, but the trees we read them under, or the cut grass we smelt as we turned the pages. What remains is a mixed impression: part text, part landscape.

This isn't a one-way relationship. If books contain miniature landscapes, they also retouch and recolour these as we read. Put less ornately, they enrich impressions, enlarge sympathies. Ivy clinging to my study window recalls Woolf's Ceylon, while pansies suggest Proust's nostalgia (there's less dodgy innuendo in their French name: *pensées*). For all my atheism, the blooms-like-clockwork *Camellia* in our front yard now suggests Voltaire's deism. The peace lily by my desk, aping an aspidistra, has Orwellian overtones.

In short, there is a continuing to-and-fro between books and gardens, which enhances both. The garden is a bookish space. With this in mind, I've written a few words on the literature that has informed or inspired this book, and my own outlook.

For all the philosophy in gardens, there is very little good modern philosophy *on* them. But David E Cooper's *A Philosophy of Gardens* (Oxford, 2006) stands out for its lucidity and sensitivity. In particular, Cooper's idea of 'exemplification' makes a good case for the particular meaning of gardens: the interdependence of nature and humanity. Cooper is also convincing on the virtues encouraged by gardens. His use of Cézanne—whose work is nicely reproduced on the cover—is particularly suggestive.

Tom Turner's *Garden History: Philosophy and Design 2000BC–2000AD* (Spon Press, 2005) combines the history of gardens, the history of ideas and a keen eye for the specifics of design. His diagrams of gardens, which give general designs and their variants, are particularly helpful. The book is expensive new, but beautifully produced.

Christopher Thacker's *The History of Gardens* (Reed, 1979) stands out for its charming prose, literary tone and relevant illustrations. It is also widely available second-hand. I enjoyed Ronald King's *The Quest for Paradise* (Mayflower Books, 1979) for the same reasons. A more comprehensive—in content and illustrations—and recent history is William Howard Adams' *Nature Perfected* (Abbeville Press, 1991). Jane Brown's *The Pursuit of Paradise* (HarperCollins, 2000) is a compelling social history of gardens. Brown's chapters on military and childhood gardens are particularly fascinating.

On the history of gardening in England, Thacker also wrote *The Genius of the Garden* (Weidenfeld & Nicolson, 1994), which combines technical details on design and planting with philosophical and literary currents. Thacker's prose is typically good. Jane Fearnley-Whittingstall's *The Garden: An English Love Affair* (Weidenfeld & Nicolson, 2002) is a detailed (and gorgeous) book, written by a practising landscape architect and garden designer. *The Genius of Place* (MIT Press, 1988), edited by John Dixon Hunt and Peter Willis, is not as well illustrated, but is a fantastic collection of historical garden documents by notable English authors, including Alexander Pope and Jane Austen.

Philosophy Alfresco

The earliest life of Aristotle is from Diogenes Laërtius' *Lives of Eminent Philosophers* (Harvard University Press, 2006). This Loeb Classical Library edition includes the original Greek as well as English (translation by RD Hicks), but cheaper translations are widely available new and second-hand. Likewise for the works of Aristotle himself. I use the two-volume Bollingen *Complete Works of Aristotle* (Princeton University Press, 1994), edited by Jonathan Barnes. The translations are good, and it is helpful to have all the works in one place. But Oxford and Penguin have cheap, well-translated editions with notes.

AN Whitehead's reference to the 'temporary laws of nature' comes from Lucien Price's *Dialogues of Alfred North Whitehead* (Max Reinhardt, 1954). While Whitehead's philosophical writings can sometimes be difficult—for their subject matter, not because he is obfuscating—his conversations are brilliant examples of the civilised art of talking and listening.

Martin Heidegger describes *physis* most clearly (for want of another word) in his essay 'The Origin of the Work of Art', in *Martin Heidegger: Basic Writings* (Routledge, 1993), edited by David Farrell Krell. Not coincidentally, Heidegger also discusses Cézanne in the same volume. Heidegger's ideas are taken up by David Cooper in his work. RG Collingwood's *The Idea of Nature* (Oxford, 1960) provides a clearer historical overview of *physis* in ancient Greece. Both books are relatively easy to find new and second-hand.

Roberto Calasso's *The Marriage of Cadmus and Harmony* (Vintage, 1994) is a brilliant meditation on myth and reality, appearance and semblance, and the nature of art (amongst other things).

The Consolations of Chawton Cottage

The day-to-day descriptions of Jane Austen come from her relatives, in *A Memoir of Jane Austen* (Wordsworth, 2007), written by James Austen-Leigh, her nephew; from her own correspondence, collected and edited by Deirdre le Faye in *Jane Austen's Letters* (Oxford, 1996); and from biographies. Of these, I most relied on Jon Spence's *Becoming Jane Austen* (Hambledon & London, 2003), and Claire Tomalin's *Jane Austen: A Life* (Penguin, 2000). Spence carefully traces Austen's romantic life, telling a plausible and often moving story of her development from flirty young miss to mature writer. Tomalin paints a bigger picture of Austen's life and era, but does so with considerable sympathy and detail. *A Portrait of Jane Austen* (BAC, 1978), by David Cecil, provides a well-illustrated character sketch of Austen and her age.

There are more editions of Austen's novels than days to read them in. I have the collected edition, published by Collector's Library in 2003. The Hugh Thomson illustrations are charming if a little twee, and the volumes are light, small and robust—perfect for portable or bedtime reading. But Austen's works can be purchased in various sizes and editions, priced for every budget.

On the critical reception of Austen, *Jane Austen: The Critical Heritage* (Routledge & Kegan Paul, 1987), edited by Brian Southam, is exhaustive, and contains some remarkable failures of taste. Gilbert Ryle's seminal essay on Austen is reproduced in *Critical Essays on*

Jane Austen (Routledge & Kegan Paul, 1978), also edited by Southam.

Alexander Pope's poems are widely available in hardback and paperback, and on the internet. Everyman (1969) does a typically robust edition of his collected poems, edited and introduced by Bonamy Dobrée, but I also have a cheap Kindle edition. His translations of Homer are particularly memorable, even today. Maynard Mack's *Alexander Pope: A Life* (WW Norton, 1986) is comprehensive on Pope's life, works and era—Mack's descriptions of England's religious backdrop are particularly illuminating. George Fraser's *Alexander Pope* (Routledge & Kegan Paul, 1978) gives a concise argument for Pope's status as a moralist. Pope's status as an author can also be understood more fully with *Pope: The Critical Heritage* (Routledge & Kegan Paul, 1973), edited by John Barnard.

Bonsai in the Bedroom

Many of the details of Proust's home and habits come from his housekeeper, Céleste Albaret, in *Monsieur Proust* (Collins & Harvill, 1976). Albaret was loyal to her employer, and perhaps a little naïve about his sexuality. But she is an invaluable source of information about Proust's rooms and routines.

Jean-Yves Tadié's *Marcel Proust: A Life* (Viking, 2000) is a landmark biography, which gives a panoramic view of Proust and his era. George D Painter's two-volume *Marcel Proust* (Penguin, 1977) lacks Tadié's up-to-date scholarship but gives a bold and dramatic portrait of the author. Richard Barker's *Marcel Proust*

(1958) is clearly written and concise, but without Tadié's factual mastery or Painter's psychological acumen. On the relationship between the younger Proust and Marie Nordlinger, *The Translation of Memory* (Peter Owen, 1999), by PF Prestwich is fascinating.

The best short, well-written story of Proust's life and work is *Proust* (Weidenfeld & Nicolson, 1999), by Edmund White. This is part of the Lives series, which also features Jane Austen, St Augustine and others—an excellent introduction to many great lives.

In his own words, Proust's *In Search of Lost Time* remains a modern classic—a unique combination of memoir, fiction, psychology and philosophy. My family owns a beautiful but heavy three-volume set by Chatto & Windus (1982), but the smaller, lighter Penguin editions are much cheaper and easier to find. His correspondence is collected in *Letters of Marcel Proust* (Helen Marx Books, 2006). Proust's non-fiction, including the essays from *Contre Sainte-Beuve*, can be read in *Marcel Proust on Art and Literature: 1896–1919* (Meridian Books, 1958).

The Apples of Monk's House

Most of the details and quotes from Leonard Woolf's long, stoical life come from his remarkable memoirs, collected in five volumes, published by the Hogarth Press: *Sowing* (1961), *Growing* (1964), *Beginning Again* (1965), *Downhill All the Way* (1967) and *The Journey Not the Arrival Matters* (1969). Woolf's correspondence, edited by Frederick Spotts in *The Letters of Leonard Woolf* (Harcourt Brace Jovanovich, 1989), is also a fascinating record of his life and century. A shorter version of Woolf's life is given in *Leonard Woolf: A Biography* (McClelland & Stewart, 2006), by Victoria Glendinning.

Woolf's first novel, *The Village in the Jungle* (The Hogarth Press, 1971) is rarely spotted new or second-hand, but I purchased a copy, in good condition, online from England.

On the marriage of Virginia and Leonard Woolf, George Spater and Ian Parsons' *A Marriage of True Minds* (Jonathan Cape & The Hogarth Press, 1977) is a fine tribute to an exceptional relationship and contains many family photos. Virginia's diaries, published in five volumes by Penguin from 1977 to 1984, and edited by Anne Oliver Bell, are intimate portraits of day-to-day life, and literature in their own right. Likewise for her sparkling letters, edited by Nigel Nicolson in six volumes, and published by Harcourt Brace Jovanovich from 1975 to 1982. Hermione Lee's biography of Virginia, *Virginia Woolf* (Chatto & Windus, 1996) also provides balance for Leonard's more personal account.

The Thought-Tree

The reference to Nietzsche's *Gedankenbaum* comes from *Friedrich Nietzsche: A Biography* (Pimlico, 2003) by Curtis Cate. Cate's work is well written, and clear on the philosopher's ideas and scholarly development. Cate tells a good yarn to boot. A more sober, but also more intellectually illuminating, biography is Rüdinger Safanski's *Nietzsche: A Philosophical Biography* (Granta, 2003). RJ Hollingdale, a noted Nietzsche translator, wrote *Nietzsche: The Man and His Work* (Routledge & Kegan Paul, 1965), which is plainly written and sympathetic (when many works on Nietzsche are obscure or fawning).

Some of the most rewarding Nietzsche scholarship in a now crowded market is by Walter Kaufman, whose *Nietzsche: Philosopher, Psychologist, Antichrist* (Princeton University Press, 1974) remains as enlightening and challenging as when it was first published.

Nietzsche's books and essays are all published widely and cheaply by Penguin, often in Hollingdale's translations. Cambridge also publishes his works, in its Cambridge Texts in the History of Philosophy series, often with helpful notes and commentaries. Amongst the most provocative and enjoyable of Nietzsche's works are his notebooks, published as *The Will to Power* (Vintage, 1968), edited by Walter Kaufman. My edition is almost dust—testament to my repeated readings, rather than the quality of the binding. Kaufman's translation of *The Gay Science* (Vintage, 1974) is also excellent.

Nietzsche's correspondence can be buoyant on one page and deflated on the next—but always fascinating. Christopher Middleton edited and translated the *Selected Letters of Friedrich Nietzsche* (University of Chicago Press, 1969). In yet another advertisement for second-hand books, my copy was owned by the American composer David Diamond and contains some marvellous marginalia ('I'd have biffed the cab owner in the mouth or nose', says Diamond's note on Nietzsche's collapse in Turin, as the philosopher watched a cabman beat his horse).

Sex and Roses

On Colette's life (and appetites), Judith Thurman's *Secrets of the Flesh: A Life of Colette* (Bloomsbury, 2000) is excellent. Thurman gives a vivid impression of the author's notoriety, without being salacious on one hand or an aloof apologist on the other. Herbert Lottman's *Colette: A Life* (Minerva, 1991) is shorter, more dramatic and certainly more fun. Germaine Greer's 'Love of Blooms', *The New York Times* 1 June 1986, is excellent on Colette's love of the "budding and the fading".

Colette's reflections on childhood, *My Mother's House* and *Sido,* are published together by Penguin (1966).

In *Earthly Paradise* (Farrar, Straus & Giroux, 1966), editor Robert Phelps brings together excerpts from Colette's autobiographical and journalistic essays. As a biography, it is limited, but it works very well as an introduction to the author's writings and ideas. Colette's writings on flowers, herbs and gardens are collected in Phelps' *Flowers and Fruit* (Farrar, Straus & Giroux, 1986).

Colette's collected works are published in the Uniform Edition (Secker & Warburg), including the classics *Claudine at School* (1956) and *Gigi/The Cat* (1958).

There are several versions of Arthur Schopenhauer's *World as Will and Idea*, but the Everyman (1995) edition, edited by David Berman, is readable and readily available.

Botanical Confessions

Over two centuries on, Rousseau's *Confessions* (Penguin, 1984) remains a startling read. The author's narcissism and delusion are oddly charming in their naivety. And he writes beautifully—simply, boldly and with an eye for anecdote. *Reveries of the Solitary Walker* (Penguin, 2004) is more paranoid, but also more lyrical, and shorter.

Most of Rousseau's main philosophical and political works are published by Penguin, though I prefer the layout and typesetting of the robust Everyman editions: *The Social Contract/Discourses* (1966) and *Émile* (1966)— I have quoted from these in the text. The treatises and essays are also published in the Cambridge Texts in the History of Political Thought series, with commentaries, notes and replies to Rousseau's contemporaries.

Rousseau is at his most calm, patient and instructive in *Botany: A Study of Pure Curiosity* (Michael Joseph, 1979), his letters to Madame Étienne Delessert. This edition also contains some exquisite illustrations by the Belgian master Pierre-Josef Redouté, court painter to Marie Antoinette.

On Rousseau's life, Maurice Cranston's three-volume biography stands out for its detail and generosity: *Jean-Jacques* (1982), *The Noble Savage* (1991) and *The Solitary Self* (1997). JH Huizinga's *Rousseau: The Self-Made Saint* (Grossman Publishers, 1976) is a more savage biography— but a good remedy for Rousseau's own conceits.

Down and Out with a Sharp Scythe

The minutiae of Orwell's day-to-day living are preserved in *Orwell: Diaries* (Harvill Secker, 2009), edited by Peter Davidson. Alongside social, political and economic observations, the entries on Orwell's Jura gardening are regular and chiefly practical (9.10.47: 'Cleared out fuchsia stump'), but they give a charming portrait of his existence (and experiments) on the island.

On Orwell's life, Jeffrey Meyers' *Orwell: Wintry Conscience of a Generation* (WW Norton & Company, 2000) is generous to the author but rightly critical of his more destructive instincts. David Lebedoff's *The Same Man* (Scribe, 2008) is a unique dual biography of Orwell and

Evelyn Waugh, which combines extensive research with fine prose, literary sympathy and a keen eye for anecdote.

Orwell's journalism and reviews are some of the finest of the twentieth century—with that of Virginia Woolf, his work exemplifies the modern essay form. These are published with Orwell's letters in four volumes by Penguin (1970), edited by Sonia Orwell and Ian Angus. *Down and Out in Paris and London* (1970) and *Burmese Days* (1978) are also published in paperback by Penguin. As with Orwell's fiction, including *Keep the Aspidistra Flying* (Penguin, 2010), all of these volumes are readily available new and second-hand, though often separately.

My edition of *1984* (Chancellor Press, 1984) is published alongside *Animal Farm*. But one of the virtues of Orwell's (late) popularity is that there are many other options for weight, cost and layout. Second-hand bookshops might sometimes be, as Orwell complained, cold, fly-blown and dusty—but they are full of his excellent writings, at Comstockian prices.

The Acres of Perhaps

Because of her continuing popularity, particularly in the United States, Emily Dickinson's poems are available in many bookshops, used and new. They are also available quickly and cheaply as ebooks. But the standard editions are more faithful and complete. The most recent standard collection is *The Poems of Emily Dickinson: Reading Edition* (The Belknap Press, 2005), edited by RW Franklin, which is a shorter edition of Franklin's earlier edition with sources. The reading edition contains all Dickinson's poems, formatted and punctuated as Dickinson left them.

An older, but also authoritative, collection was edited by Thomas Johnson (Faber & Faber, 1976).

The standard edition of Dickinson's letters—often literally tied up with the poet's flowers—is the two-volume *Letters of Emily Dickinson* (The Belknap Press, 1958), edited by Johnson and Theodora Ward. A cheaper and less reliable collection, edited by Mabel Loomis Todd, is published by Dover (2003). This still gives a good glimpse of the poet's life and ideas, in her own words.

Alfred Habegger's *My Wars Are Laid Away in Books: The Life of Emily Dickinson* (The Modern Library, 2001) is a superb biography, which gives a gripping and psychologically penetrating portrait of the poet. Lyndall Gordon's *Lives Like Loaded Guns* (Virago Press, 2011) shows how Dickinson's legacy, and public reputation, was changed by continuing family conflicts. On Dickinson and gardens, Judith Farr's *The Gardens of Emily Dickinson* (Harvard University Press, 2004) is excellent—not only on the poet's horticultural habits, but also on their relationship to her poems, social life and ideas.

Raking Stones

Nikos Kazantzakis was a committed and curious traveller, who sent many reflections home to his second wife, Eleni Samios. She collected these and others, with her own commentary, in *Nikos Kazantzakis: A Biography Based on his Letters* (Cassirer, 1968). He also wrote extensively on his travels, including *Japan China* (Simon & Schuster, 1963), *England* (Cassirer, 1965), *Spain* (Simon & Schuster, 1963) and *Journeying* (Little, Brown & Co., 1975). His time in Japan and China was also fictionalised in *The Rock Garden* (Simon & Schuster, 1963). Many of these are difficult to find new but can be found online second-hand.

The *Odyssey: A Modern Sequel* (Secker & Warburg, 1959) is a poetic version of Kazantzakis' process philosophy. Translated with punch by Kimon Friar, it remains the fullest expression of Kazantzakis' ideas. Simon & Schuster (1958) also does a cheap, readily available paperback edition. Kazantzakis' friend, Cretan author Pandelis Prevelakis, wrote a critical but sympathetic study of the poem, *Nikos Kazantzakis and The Odyssey* (Simon & Schuster, 1961).

Kazantzakis also outlined his philosophy in *The Saviors of God: Spiritual Exercises* (Simon & Schuster, 1960) and parts of his memoir, *Report to Greco* (Simon & Schuster, 1965)—a masterwork of fictionalised autobiography, alongside classics like Rousseau's *Confessions*.

On Kazantzakis' life and work, Peter Bien's two-volume *Politics of the Spirit* (Princeton University Press, 1989 & 2007) is an immense contribution. Investigating the author's ideas, politics and art, and their relationships, it draws on decades of research to present a convincing portrait of Kazantzakis. It is not a simple read, but it is a compelling one.

Chestnuts and Nothingness

Sartre's *Nausea* (Penguin, 1965) is not a systematic treatise, but it is a better introduction to existentialism than *Being and Nothingness* (Philosophical Library, 1956). The point is not that Sartre's opus is bad philosophy—not at all. The point is that it is badly written, and fails to invite readers into existentialism's transformative worldview. Having said this, *Being and Nothingness*'s passages on slime alone are worth the price of admission—to say nothing of the author's defence of free consciousness.

'The Humanism of Existentialism' is from *Essays in Existentialism* (Citadel Press, 1974), edited by Wade Baskin, as are other short essays and excerpts. Sartre's essay on the sculptor Alberto Giacometti is particularly memorable for its description of the 'promise' of the statues—their unreachable solidity.

Ronald Hayman's *Writing Against: A Biography of Sartre* (Weidenfeld & Nicolson, 1986) is a broad portrait of the philosopher, which skilfully binds philosophy, politics and the personal. Sartre's own memoir, *Words* (Hamish Hamilton, 1964), is more biased, but no less fascinating for this. *Sartre: The Philosopher of the Twentieth Century* (Polity, 2003), by Bernard-Henri Lévy, is an illuminating and often witty investigation of the philosopher's life, work and era. Lévy is particularly revealing on Sartre's longing to escape himself, for all his defence of freedom.

Sartre's journals from World War II show Sartre, in his thirties, coping with the boredom, class politics and absurdity of war. They also reveal the development of Sartre's philosophy up to *Being and Nothingness*, including notes on Heidegger, authenticity and history. They are collected in *The War Diaries of Jean-Paul Sartre: November 1939–March 1940* (Pantheon Books, 1984), edited by his adopted daughter, Arlette Alkaïm-Sartre.

Some of Sartre's letters are as dramatic, keen-eyed and funny as his fiction. Many of his best are contained in *Witness to My Exile: The Letters of Jean-Paul Sartre to Simone de Beauvoir 1926–1939* (Charles Scribner's

Sons, 1993), edited by de Beauvoir herself. Her replies are in *Simone de Beauvoir: Letters to Sartre* (Vintage, 1992), edited by Quinton Hoare. The early years of their love and friendship, including Sartre's stay in Le Havre, are recorded in de Beauvoir's *The Prime of Life* (Penguin, 1981). The late Hazel Rowley's recent portrait of the couple, *Tête-à-Tête* (Chatto & Windus, 2006) is light on their work but heavy on their romantic cruelties. It also shows de Beauvoir's loyalty to Sartre—and his desperate need of it.

The Best of All Possible Estates

This chapter was first suggested by Adam Gopnik's elegant essay 'Voltaire's Garden', in the *New Yorker*, 7 March 2005.

John Pearson's *Voltaire Almighty: A Life in Pursuit of Freedom* (Bloomsbury, 2005) gives a full depiction of Voltaire's era, personality and ideas. Pearson reveals the great author's faults and relationships without being snarky or gossipy. Richard Aldington's *Voltaire* (Chatto & Windus, 1935) lacks Pearson's depth and breadth but is intelligent and often pithy.

In *Voltaire* (Weidenfeld & Nicolson, 1986), AJ Ayer offers a sharp analysis of Voltaire's philosophical ideas and debates, and is not afraid to judge Voltaire's literature ('Voltaire's tragedies were melodramas and like over-cooked soufflés they have fallen flat').

Voltaire's literary and philosophical works are readily available in French and translation, on paper and in electronic editions. Everyman (1962) has a good collection of *Candide* and other tales, though Three Sirens Press (1930) has a striking stand-alone edition, illustrated by Mahlon Blaine. *A Pocket Philosophical Dictionary* (Oxford, 2011) has a reader-friendly layout and contains two contemporary portraits of Voltaire. I also have a free electronic edition, which lacks the introduction and appendices, but is a workable translation and can be searched quickly. My copy of Voltaire's *Philosophical Letters* (Hackett, 2007) is also electronic, but it is not difficult to find in paperback by Penguin, published as *Letters on England* (1980).

A Stranger at the Gates

There are many good editions of Plato's dialogues. I have the *Collected Dialogues* (Princeton University Press, 1996), edited by Edith Hamilton and Huntington Cairns. This includes the letters and an excellent index. But Plato's works are widely available in cheap paperbacks new and second-hand, and in ebook formats. While away from my home library, I also bought an ebook edition of Plato and Aristotle's collected works—it cost less than the coffee I was drinking.

Acknowledgements

Many thanks to Scribe UK's Philip Gwyn Jones for championing my work; to Molly Slight for always having the right answers to my bewildered questions; to Allison Colpoys for making yet another gorgeous cover; and to Mick Pilkington and Kevin O'Brien for turning unruly data into a handsome book.

I'm grateful to Sharon Galant and Benython Oldfield from Zeitgeist Media for their support and encouragement. Without whom …

Many thanks also to my local publishers, MUP: Elisa Berg for commissioning this book, and for her generous editorial support; Sally Heath for her counsel; Sarah Bailey for her copyediting wizardry; Penelope White for her editorial stewardship; and Trisha Garner for her lovely cover design.

Illustrator Dan Keating has (again) been a joy to work with: a rare combination of artistry, intellect and armbars.

Thanks also to Ian Britain, Christopher Lawrence, and Margaret Connolly for timely advice and feedback. Glyn Davis was always encouraging. And Sandra Price deserves thanks for suggesting a chapter on Colette.

I'm grateful to Arts Victoria and Melbourne University's Writing Centre for Scholars and Researchers for financial assistance. Thanks also to Simon Clews for his ongoing support.

I'm obliged to the Jane Austen Societies of Australia and Melbourne for letting me debut my Austen chapter with such a hospitable audience. Particular thanks to Susannah Fullerton, Andrea Richards and the late Jon Spence, a gentleman and scholar.

The following assisted generously with technical information: Carl Kelson and Mike Blackburn from Victrack; Andrew Gay, Property and Campus Services (Asset Services), University of Melbourne; arborist Greg Mitchell, Whitehorse City Council. Thanks also to Emma Darwin for her impressions of St James's Park.

I'm indebted to Eike Schmidt, chief Decorative Arts Curator at the Minneapolis Institute of Arts, for his translation of Jacob Björnståhl. Thanks also to Dr Chris Andrews for passing along the translation of Proust's Noailles review; to Professor David Leatherbarrow for his illuminating work on Shaftesbury; and to Varvara Tsaka from Crete's Nikos Kazantzakis Museum for photos of Kazantzakis.

David Lebedoff has been fine company on this philosophical and literary journey—one day we will actually meet in person.

Thank you to my parents and mother-in-law for kid-wrangling while I worked at the cafe. Every hour helped.

Nikos and Sophia put up with my exile for the last few weeks of this manuscript. Kids: I'll be back to classroom help and kindergarten duty very soon. And to my beloved Ruth, thank you for your love, trust, scholarship—and mowing.